REFLECTIONS

DENNIS A. MCINTYRE

Books may be ordered through booksellers or by contacting:
Bennett Media and Marketing
1603 Capitol Ave., Suite 310 A233
Cheyenne, WY 82001
www.thebennettmediaandmarketing.com
Phone: 1-307-202-9292

ISBN: 978-1-964296-14-2 (softcover)
ISBN: 978-1-964296-15-9 (eBook)

Printed in the United States of America

REFLECTIONS

Contents

Preface   VII

1. On The Road Again   1

2. Therapy   11

3. The Message   23

4. P.E.P.   31

5. The Coffee Shop   45

6. The Follow Up   59

7. Rick's Meeting   75

8. The Old Stomping Ground   87

9. Cranberry Pond   97

10. Witnessing   103

11. One Last Stop   109

12. The Return Trip   121

13. The Letter   131

14. Final Reflection   137

Epilogue   147

Preface

The road of Life is unique for every individual. Millions of decisions are made through each change in direction or event. Retracing our steps would be an impossible task. At best, we might recall the major events that made a difference in our lives or the lives of others. Travelling back to those places where our journey began may provide some answers to one question, "Has my life made a difference?"

As we near the end of our time on earth, another question may enter our minds. "Is this the end or is there more?" As a Christian, my hope is on eternity and a glorious reunion with friends and family. "Who will be there to greet me in heaven?" Reflecting on that question takes me on one more journey. Perhaps, the trip will provide some answers.

On The Road Again

T ravelling back to his birthplace seemed like a good idea. Donny's wife of nearly forty years passed away in two thousand seven. The last time that he made the trip to upstate New York was for her eulogy. She had kept many friendships there over the years as the church was full that day. That was seventeen years ago. Donny's life had been blessed with a successful engineering career, children, grandchildren, great grandchildren and many friends. Now it was time to make the trip north as a time of reflection. He hopes to reacquaint with friends and family once again before the time comes when God calls him to rejoin his wife in heaven.

Leaving his empty house was never a problem after her passing. The silence was deafening. Often the television was on just for the sound, while Donny completed crosswords or challenging math puzzles. Writing was also therapy. He had composed many stories about everyday people that crossed his path over the years. Looking back, Donny could see the hand of God on his life. Many of his readers insisted that his stories were divine appointments.

He thought about those words a lot. He also wondered why God would take his wife. Perhaps, he would not have started writing if she lived. The thought that God desired to use him to reach others offered solace. Perhaps, he would find new answers to his questions on the trip north.

One or two days per week involved a round of golf with a group of men. Local coffee houses offered places of refuge as well. Still, Donny was overwhelmed with feelings and thoughts about where life had taken him, why his wife had to leave so soon and why he was still here. He had committed his life to follow his savior Jesus Christ at the age of twenty-five. His children and grandchildren were also devoted Christians, so that part of his life held a measure of success. He hoped that the ride north would provide a time of further reflection and help to answer the many questions that filled his head. One thing he knew for certain. He was not about to embark alone. God had been with him through all the trials in his life and would be his travelling companion now.

As Donny hit the road thoughts of his father came to his mind. The two of them had made the trip from Florida, where his father lived, many times in the past especially after mom died. Golf clubs were always packed and the Carolinas provided ample places to enjoy a round together. Donny would fly to Orlando, where dad would meet him at the airport. Off they would go. The trip allowed dad to have a vehicle during his stay. At the end of the trip, the process would reverse, providing another round of golf followed by a returned flight back home. Those trips were always made while Donny's wife was alive. Dad enjoyed being with family and visiting old friends. Still, the ride with just a father and his son was special indeed.

Since Donny did all of the driving, dad did crosswords, played road games and wrote down license plate information. At the end of the trip he would count all of the different states represented. On one trip the number was forty-one, including Hawaii and Alaska. As Donny began driving a Texas plate caught his eye, and he could almost see his dad smiling. Without the memory created with dad, the plate would have just passed by without even a thought. Little things would trigger great memories from those trips. Our memories are unique. Things that may seem inconsequential become giant road signs to Donny. He found himself observing every license plate and smiled when a new state appeared.

As Donny entered the Carolinas, road signs began to trigger more memories. As he approached a familiar golf course some events popped up in his head. One of them involved a morning round. It was July or August, since dad wanted to escape the hot months in Florida. Pulling into the golf course seemed strange as only three or four cars were in the parking lot. The normal four and one-half-hour round of golf took less than three hours and they hit the road home once more. It was noon. Donny remembers the time well as a large time-temperature clock was on a road sign. The temperature was one-hundred-five degrees Fahrenheit. When Donny shared that story with his wife upon return he got a tongue-lashing. "Your dad is eighty years old. You can't take him out in that heat."

Donny remembers the look on his father's face while she rebuked her husband. Dad thought it was funny and we laughed. With no one on the golf course we never felt the heat. The wind passed through the cart with refreshment. The round would have been unbearable if we had to wait on every hole played, but that didn't happen. The car air conditioning offered quick relief as well. Passing that course seemed to bring a wry smile to Donny's face. How precious are those memories that still make us smile. When we relive those moments, we feel the presence of those who are no longer with us. What a blessing, indeed.

On one return trip back to Florida Donny stopped around four o'clock in the afternoon to fill up. Dad thought it was for another reason and yelled "Looking for a golf course?" Donny smiled and proceeded to pull into a gas station. After going in to make the payment, Donny inquired about the location of the nearest golf course. The attendant said that there was one less than a mile away and off they went. Donny did not recall very much about the course but the hours afterwards brought a smile to his face. It was still light so Donny decided to drive further south before looking for a motel for the night. After reaching dad's apartment the next day, dad suggested playing bridge before Donny had to catch his return flight. Duplicate bridge was a card game played with partners, four to a table. East-West teams moved every three hands played to the next table with new opponents. Dad used that in an attempt to trigger responses from the new players. The conversation went something like this:

Dad: "How would you like to be dragged five-hundred miles, forced to play golf and then drive another three hours before stopping."

Card player: "Really?"

Dad expected a much better response, so the next team would hear: "How would you like to be dragged six-hundred miles, forced to play golf and then drive another three hours before stopping."

Donny enjoyed the lack of genuine concern for his father's attempts to solicit compassion. By the time the bridge session was over the miles were over a thousand with no comments like, "That's too bad" or "I am so sorry for you." Although dad may have welcomed such responses, Donny sensed the humor his dad seemed to enjoy through the sharing. Just thinking about those times made the trip north pass quickly.

A Dunkin Donuts sign captured Donny's eye as well. Donny would welcome the opportunities to treat dad to nice dinners, while dad insisted of paying for a donut stop. Travelling down to Florida to spend time with dad always involved a local establishment. As a regular customer dad knew where the donut deals were and made sure that it was his treat. Later that evening, Donny paid for dinner at a more exclusive restaurant. Dad usually had steak. His smile made the meal special.

Donny wished that he had the means for much higher financial gifts for his father, but those steak dinners were like gold. It had been well over twenty years since his father's passing yet, somehow, the donut sign made it seem like dad was right there with him. He stopped, ordered coffee and one blueberry friedcake. That was dad's favorite. "This is for you dad," he thought, as he left the establishment.

Donny's thoughts seemed to focus on his father in remembrance of all those rides together. Wax beans suddenly popped into his head. The south was known for green beans, but upstate New York had a yellow variety, which had special significance. During his teen years Donny worked for various farmers near their home. Normally, he would earn seventy-five cents per hour hoeing or picking tomatoes. But picking yellow or green beans was unique. One farmer offered thirty-five cents per peck basket and Donny could pick five baskets an hour. It was a huge bonus. Dad also grew yellow beans in his garden. When they got picked we ate a special meal together. Dad grew up near or on a farm and meat was rare. Vegetables were staples. A large pot of boiled potatoes and yellow beans were cooked and drained. Then they were strained and mixed with whole milk. Butter, pepper and other seasonings were added. Then the mixture was reheated. The result was a meal to die for. Even after seconds, there was more than enough for another meal. Donny could almost taste it as he drove.

On one trip back to Florida, darkness began to set in near the Georgia-Florida border. A peck basket of yellow beans was loaded into a grocery bag prior to leaving Upstate New York. The sunlight was nearly gone. Dad put aside his crossword book and grabbed the bag. Then, he reached into his pants pocket and pulled out a small fishing knife. By the time they entered Florida, a bag of small yellow bean pieces was ready for cooking, Dad suggested stopping at the first store to buy the remaining ingredients. We arrived at his apartment late and had the delicious meal around two in the morning. What a way to end the long drive. You might think that Donny would be too tired from driving, but that was not the case.

Following the dinner, he slept like a baby. He also had at least two more meals before catching his flight back.

The road was clear and the clouds were like puffs of cotton. Donny could not remember a trip with his dad that was stormy. The trips were always in the summer, so winter snow and ice were not present. Nevertheless, it seemed strange to not have any memory of bad conditions. Pennsylvania offered new thoughts in remembrance to those trips. Conversations with dad seemed to center around being with family and friends. Donny could use the cell phone technology to initiate conversations, but those trips with dad lacked them. He pondered such a trip on this day and how things might be different with those technical interruptions. Then he let God know how thankful he was for those times alone with his father.

Rochester was an industrial city where companies like Eastman Kodak and Xerox held prominence. Donny worked as an electrical engineer at Kodak during several of the trips with dad. Driving back offered thoughts about past employment and various sites. He couldn't wait to enjoy a Friday fish fry with a cod fillet completely covering the plate. Rochester was also known for the best BBQ chicken wings, Zweigle's hot dogs and Abbotts custard. Anyone, familiar with the area would know what these are to be sure. Still, thoughts of resampling these things were heavy on

Donny's mind. As Donny drove through the city several land-marks had replaced those he remembered. The buildings that he worked in were reduced to parking lots. Some sadness was felt.

He looked forward to sharing with his younger brother Jason who still lived in the area. Jason recently retired and lived by Lake Ontario with his wife, daughter and grandson. Moving south had limited visits over the years but this trip hoped to change all that. The fourteen-hour trip seemed to go by quickly as the memories of the past consumed his thoughts.

Therapy

Donny called Jason as he neared his home. It was too late to suggest dinner but the thought of a custard sounded like a better idea. Jason met him at an Abbotts close to his home and they shared the treat together. After a long ride it was just the thing Donny needed. Chocolate-almond custard on a waffle cone was a specialty to die for. A hand-packed pint was also taken home for the rest of the family to enjoy as well. The two brothers shared retirement issues and then departed for Jason's house.

Jason seemed to be more interested in sharing things about his grandson Jacob who was asleep when we arrived. Prior to retirement, Jason worked at home a lot. That allowed him to be around Jacob more than his three other grandchildren who lived with their parents on the other side of town. Retirement offered even more time to be with Jacob and, perhaps, with the rest of his family. Jason's wife Erica was also asleep. The living room couch became Donny's bed for the evening. The smell of bacon seemed to excite Donny's senses as he awoke the next day. Erica and Jason were up.

Donny: "Good morning, Erica."

Erika: "Good morning, Donny. "Breakfast will be ready shortly. I hope you are hungry."

Donny: "I normally just have coffee but bacon and eggs smells really good."

Erika: "Jason is in the back yard."

Donny: "I thought he retired and would be sleeping in."

Erika: "He usually gets up to watch the sunrise but retirement just means that he can take a nap in the afternoon."

Donny smiled and dismissed himself to get cleaned up. Then he went to the back yard to call Jason for breakfast. Jacob and his mother Mary joined them. Donny offered prayer and then Jacob added another "amen." It was a warm touch. Jacob was six or seven years old, but seemed much older. He had a wonderful way with words and always seemed to have a smile on his face. Donny could see the joy on everyone's faces.

Breakfast was more than just a great meal. Donny had not visited his brother since his wife died and the reunion was special. Although Jacob seemed to be the center of attention, Donny could sense a warm family embrace. His mind went back to the time when he was the age of Jacob in a foster home where he did not feel loved. The setting with Jason's family warmed his heart and made the trip north seem special as well. There was something about the time with family that touched his soul to the core. God was with him, and he could not wait for all that will occur during the week. It was Friday and the thought of a fish fry filled Donny's mind.

Donny: "Do they still have those great Friday fish fries?"

Mary: "They sure do Uncle Donny. I must go to work but I would love to join you later."

Jason: "The closest restaurant also sells the custard we had last night."

Donny: "That settles it then. What time would be good for you, Mary?"

Mary: "Any time after five is good for me."

Donny: "I remember those Friday nights and the crowds. Can we agree on five o'clock?"

Jason: "That works. I know Mary will be here before then, but she can meet us there if she's late."

Donny: "I'm treating, bro."

Jason: "I'll get the custard to go. Those fish fries are pretty big and you won't be hungry for a cone afterwards."

Donny smiled. Jason set up a checkers game and invited Jacob to play. After several games, Jason asked Donny to challenge the winner. Jacob won and then skillfully held his own once more.

Donny: "Jacob, you play very well."

Jason: "He usually beats me two out of three."

Jacob: "Papa lets me win sometimes."

Donny: "I watched you play and I don't think your grandpa lets you win."

Jason: "That's for sure. I taught him too well."

Donny: "You are a very smart boy, Jacob."

Jacob smiled. The conversation triggered an incident that occurred about thirty years ago, when Jason had a serious skiing accident on White Face Mountain in the Adirondacks. The family had escaped for a vacation. Erica and Mary went shopping while Jason and his son Joel hit the slopes. What started as a time of family fun quickly turned to near disaster. Joel was skiing ahead when he saw one of his father's skis pass him down the slope. He looked back and saw Jason slide head first into a brick structure. Fear instantly gripped his heart as he raced to help his father. By the time he reached him the sound of a helicopter hovered over the slope. His father was airlifted to the nearest hospital. Joel went with him.

Erica had left a number where she could be reached when the guys were done skiing. Joel made the call with the sad news. Erica then made several calls to various prayer groups from her church and others. Donny's family was included.

Erica: "Jason is unconscious with massive head swelling from a skiing accident. The doctors are not very optimistic."

Donny: "I will pray for him and your family. I will also solicit other prayer warriors."

Erica: "Thank you. I guess this is in God's hands now. I feel helpless."

Donny: "Try not to worry too much. We will drive up tomorrow. I pray for God's comfort to surround you, Mary and Joel."

It was a four-hour drive the next day. Upon leaving Donny sought the Lord's help. He asked questions like, "What words could be said to console?" or "What could he do to help ease the tension?" Then, a wee small voice brought comfort. Upon arriving at the hospital Erica was there to meet them. Her eyes showed signs of intense crying.

Donny: "Jason is coming out of his coma within three days."

Erica: "The doctors here said that his head injury is extremely severe and that the coma aids in the healing process."

Donny: "That may be true, but a small voice ensured me that it would be only three days. That gave me great relief as I made this trip. I think it came from God."

Erica: "I must say that I have my doubts and concerns but I have had those wee voice messages before as well. "

Donny: "There's something else that I need to share about that voice. Jason will be made whole again."

Erica: "The doctors describe a long convalescent period to regain general functions like talking, eating and walking to name a few. The chances that Jason will be able to return to working as a computer programmer again were extremely poor."

Donny: "That's what I am trying to share with you Erica. Jason will return to work as before. I do not know the time it might take but that was the message that I received."

Erica led them up to the ward where Jason was resting. Donny went in and saw his brother under an oxygen tent with various tubes providing the medicines and food needed. Bandages wrapped most of his head. If it had not been for that wee small voice, the scene may have been unbearable. Donny stood beside his bed and bowed in prayer thanking God. During the initial conversation with Erica the conditions around the accident were shared. The helicopter service had been instituted for the first time that very day. Jason was the first patient. Donny thought that was no accident in itself. The words Donny shared brought comfort that only God could provide. Somehow, Donny knew that the seemingly lifeless body hidden under the covering would not remain that way for long.

That evening the neurosurgeon shared that the swelling in Jason's head had significantly reduced. It was the first major sign they were hoping for. They assured everyone that he was still critical but that the longer that process took, the greater the chance for irrevocable damage to the brain could occur. Somehow, Donny knew that God had intervened.

The following afternoon Erica came out to the waiting room with excitement.

Erica: "Jason is awake. He is awake."

Donny: "You sound surprised."

Erica: "I may have expected him to regain consciousness but not this soon."

Donny: "That voice was so real that I knew it would happen just as told."

Just as the doctors shared, Jason needed help to regain simple bodily functions. His voice was slurred and unrecognizable. IVs were needed to provide the necessary nourishment. The hospital was not equipped to help with special brain recuperation functions, which would be required after the other basic needs were reestablished. They discussed airlifting him to a Rochester hospital that could better meet those needs. That idea was quickly scrapped for fear of harming the head cavity with pressure changes from such a flight. Jason was released within a week and transported by ambulance to the Rochester hospital. It was nothing less than a miracle.

Donny began visiting Jason regularly at the hospital, which was a short drive from his home. Was this a God thing? Donny would agree that it was. He watched his brother tackle the concept of eating with utensils, standing on one leg and many other tests in his rehabilitation processes. Jason was told that he would need to get special follow up sessions with cognitive functions even after he would be released from the hospital. Once he was able to feed himself, speak with clarity and stand of one leg for two minutes, he would be able to recuperate at home.

As a way for Jason to gain the use of his hands, Donny brought a deck of playing cards to the hospital. A tray was placed over his bed, which was cranked up to a vertical position. The game was gin rummy, which they had played many times before the accident. One rule was that the loser of each hand dealt the next one. Jason did a lot of dealing that also involved shuffling the cards. Each future visit started with the same words.

> Donny: "It's time for your therapy session, brother."

> Jason: (with a smile) "Cut the cards. Remember, low card deals."

Jason was able to master something that resembled card shuffling and dealing, but initially had difficulty sorting the cards properly. As a result he found himself exercising his hands and fingers often. Win or lose it was a time of enjoyment and a break from the mundane time spent in the hospital.

The doctors thought that the process of rehabilitation would take a year or longer, with the more challenging work on the brain to follow afterwards. To their surprise Jason was still standing on one foot after ten minutes one day. It was evidence that equilibrium had returned. Jason even marveled at the accomplishment. They allowed Jason to recuperate at home after only a month at the hospital. They wanted him to consider the brain exercises with a professional but that never happened. Jason went back to work in his computer field soon afterwards. God had provided the healing and the doctors called Jason their living miracle.

Donny enjoyed talking to Jacob. He was a smart little boy who loved his grandpa. Thoughts of Jason's skiing accident brought the past into the forefront. He could have died that day and never enjoyed the pleasure of playing checkers with his grandson. Donny wondered if Jacob even knew about that day. Probably not, he thought.

While Jacob went into the kitchen to help Erica make cookies, Donny made a request to Jason.

Donny: "Are you ready for your therapy bro?"

Jason: "Bring it on. Cut the cards. Low card deals."

Donny had played gin rummy with his father as a teenager and then all through life. Now, the only time he played was with his brother. The idea of it being therapy, was no longer the issue as the games were on an equal playing field.

The Message

V isiting the hometown brought on other memories. A Free Methodist church was part of the family's Sunday morning ritual, so it was on Donny's list to revisit. He had many pastors in the pulpit over the years while his children were growing up but had a special remembrance for two of them. One was Pastor Gates who performed their wedding ceremony on August 17, 1968. The date was significant as the requested date was to be the following Saturday the twenty-fourth. Pastor Gates asked if they could move the date back as his family had scheduled a vacation starting that weekend. Since the time was months away they agreed to the new date.

Significant dates and events often direct future paths when we reflect back. The wedding went as planned along with a week in the Pocono Mountains in Pennsylvania for the honeymoon. Life was to begin anew where two became one. The following Sunday morning provided a life changing moment. Pastor Gates died on the twenty-fourth. His passing seemed to penetrate Donny and his wife's soul to the core. The canoe that he and his son were in had capsized. He tried to save his son and drowned in the process. His son survived. The very day that was selected for the wedding had become a sad one indeed. Contemplating all of the "What if?" questions seemed fruitless. What did ring out loud and clear was the thought that his passing must have had a reason. Whenever Donny and his wife quarreled, reconciliation always came through the thought that their marriage began with significance. Pastor Gates was no longer here on earth but his spirit ministered to two hearts for a lifetime.

A second pastor provided a significant event in Donny's life. Although he does not remember the pastor's name, his message struck a chord. It was titled "They're Not Trees." It seemed like a strange title for a sermon. What did he mean? Donny remembers a time when his teenage son was shooting hoops in the driveway one evening. It was Thursday or rather garbage collection day. Donny had placed the trash receptacles near the road for pickup that morning. When he arrived home the empty containers were still there. Although that was part of the normal events for the week, something made Donny yell to his son.

Donny: "Jeff. Why didn't you put the empty trash containers back in the garage?"

Jeff: "I didn't see them dad."

Donny: "I can't believe you said that. Please put them in the garage."

Jeff: "Sure, dad."

From that day on, Jeff made sure that the task was completed every Thursday while he was home. The words from that sermon struck a note. Until that day the empty containers were like trees. His son was unaware that they existed. The message from the sermon was clear. Christians need to make themselves aware of their environment. People and situations are far more than trees.

To explain the sermon from the pastor's perspective, he used the example of a new car. He asked the congregation to remember the first time they had purchased a new vehicle. He then asked them to remember what they saw driving out of the dealer's lot. Overwhelmingly, the response was a surprising number of cars like the one they just purchased. Those cars had always been there but now became visible through the image of the car they now owned. The message was simple but effective.

Donny made it a point to identify people, events and conditions as Jesus might see them. Over the years, he paid for coffee or meals when he sensed that someone was hungry or thirsty but without the means to pay for the items. The look of sadness might solicit conversation with a stranger. Often, God would supply the words needed that provided uplifting relief. At times, witnesses would approach Donny with words like "That was nice of you." Donny did not remember responding but thought it was sad that others did not see the hunger or ignored it.

Often, sermons seem to penetrate the hearts of people in a congregation as if the message was intended only for them. Donny's heart was deeply moved over fifty years ago. Perhaps, the sermon had touched other hearts as well but it certainly changed Donny's view of the world. He spent five years with his brothers in several foster homes after his biological mother died. Some of the foster homes left scars of abuse. He was eight when dad remarried and they became a family again. For much of his early life, Donny felt deprived of parental love. His childhood scars resurfaced after he married and began raising a family. He sought help from his eternal father to be the best parent possible. Those feelings and emotions from his childhood became like a sixth sense for others in similar experiences throughout his life. For Donny, those people with emotional issues whom entered his adult life were recognized. To Donny they were not trees.

One verse in Ephesians captured Donny's mind and heart during his wife's battle with cancer.

Ephesians 2:10 (KJV)

For we are his workmanship, created in Christ Jesus unto good works, which God had before ordained that we should walk in them.

God had a plan for Donny from the beginning. Whatever life had dealt him was for a reason. God had a plan for him and it involved good works. Other biblical accounts began to have special meaning as well.

Mark 5: 25-34 (KJV)

25. And a certain woman, which had an issue of blood twelve years,

26. And had suffered many things of many physicians, and had spent all that she had, and was nothing bettered, but rather grew worse,

27. When she had heard of Jesus, came in the press behind, and touched his garment.

28. For she said, If I may touch but his clothes, I shall be whole.

29. And straightway the fountain of her blood was dried up; and she felt in her body that she was healed of that plague.

*30. And Jesus, immediately knowing in himself that virtue had gone out of him, turned him around in the press, and said, **Who touched my clothes?***

*31. And his disciples said unto him, Thou seest the multitude thronging thee, and sayest thou, **Who touched me?***

32. And he looked around to see her that had done this thing.

33. But the woman fearing and trembling, knowing what was done in her, came and fell down before him, and told him all the truth.

34. And he said unto her, Daughter, thy faith hath made thee whole; go in peace, and be whole of thy plague.

The woman had suffered for a long time and exhausted all earthly sources. She believed that Jesus could heal her if only to touch his garment. Jesus knew, immediately, that the healing flowed to her. Jesus was fully aware of his surroundings. His senses are much more acute than any human. He knew that the woman's faith had been rewarded and healing power flowed from him. The woman was not a tree.

The pastor in his message also used the parable of the Good Samaritan in Luke 10. A priest and Levite saw a beaten man and passed by on the other side. They were considered more righteous than the Samaritan who stopped to help the man. He did not see a tree and had compassion. The Jewish community despised Samaritans. Jesus made it a point to show that loving your neighbor went beyond those who were familiar. In verse thirty-seven Jesus commanded the disciples to show mercy and go and do likewise.

P.E.P.

Donny left for church on Sunday morning. It was a warm sunny drive about ten minutes away. The two-story brick building became a familiar site as he turned into the parking area. He was married in a much smaller church about a mile away. Now, the old church was a converted paint store. The last service that he attended there had an easel near the front entrance. Perched on it was a drawing of Pastor Gate's dream for a new church, which was well into the planning stage. The brick building was very close to the artist's drawing. Donny could not help smiling as he pictured Pastor Gates enjoying the scene with him. The parking lot was more than half full so he thought that he might see many of his old friends. One of them was a retired pastor who recognized Donny and met him at the door.

Pastor: "Donny. What a pleasant surprise to see you."

Donny: "I hoped to see some old friends here Pastor

Rick. You're the first. Except for a few more gray hairs, you look the same."

Pastor Rick: "I think there are more than a few gray hairs. It looks like you have lost a few."

Donny: "The top is pretty thin."

Pastor Rick: "Don't worry. I am not preaching today."

Donny: "That's a relief," (said with a wry smile)

Pastor Rick: "What brings you here?"

Donny: "You know that I lost my wife and have retired."

Pastor Rick: "I attended her eulogy here. That was special."

Donny: "She was special as well. After seventeen years, I decided to take the trip north, perhaps for the last time."

Pastor Rick: "I hope that is not the case. You have been such an encourager to me."

Donny: "I remember you sharing with me that you thought I had the spiritual gift of encouragement. I also denied it back then."

Pastor Rick: "What about now, Donny?"

Donny: "A lot has happened since. We can talk about that after the service if you like?"

Pastor Rick: "I would love that. Please join my wife and I for lunch; our treat."

Donny: "That would be great but you don't have to pay."

Pastor Rick: "It would be my pleasure. We have a lot to talk about."

Donny went inside and sat near the front with the pastor and his wife. He looked around as he entered and recognized a few friends. After the service one family came over, whom Donny did not remember, and introduced themselves.

Jerry: "You probably don't remember me Donny. My name is Jerry Thompson. This is my wife Karen and our three children, Joey, Michelle and Adam. You may remember my mom Lisa."

Donny: "The name sounds familiar."

Jerry: "You may remember giving me driving lessons over thirty years ago."

Donny: "Now I remember. Your mom was the strawberry lady."

Jerry: "That's right."

Karen: "Strawberry lady?"

Donny: "She decorated her kitchen with strawberry wallpaper and stencils. She loved that room."

Karen: I never knew Jerry's mother. She died of cancer before we met."

Jerry: "Donny came over to the house to replace the

electrical service when mom's cancer came back. She had been in remission for several years before that."

Donny: "I had to delay that work one week as Lisa invited me in for coffee. I sensed something was wrong when I arrived."

Jerry: "I wasn't there that day, but you came over a lot after that. We started attending church with you."

Donny: "How's your older brother doing?"

Jerry: "David lives about twenty miles south with his wife and family. Our families have accepted Christ as our savior and are close."

With those words Donny could not hold back the tears. He hugged Jerry and Karen. The events of that day when he arrived at Lisa's home began to resurface. Donny remembered singing hymns over Lisa with many church members at her bedside just before she passed. He remembered Lisa moving her lips as if she could sing along but no sound came out. Over the years Donny's daughter had kept in touch with Jerry and his family. Now, Donny could put the face with the name and was thrilled to meet his family. Lisa may have been looking down with pride as well.

Several others in the congregation introduced themselves. Most of them were children whose parents had passed away. Donny felt sad but remembered them. Then he left to meet Pastor Rick for lunch at a familiar restaurant nearby.

Pastor Rick: "So Donny. What did you think of the service?"

Donny: "I used to sing bass here in the choir so I am glad to hear them sing today."

Pastor Rick: "They could use you even now."

Donny: "I sing in a large choir with an orchestra back in Georgia. You would love it Pastor."

Pastor Rick: "I am sure I would."

Donny: "We sing a lot of hymns and only a few contemporary songs. Our music director is really great."

Pastor Rick: "So what about the sermon today?"

Donny: "To be honest Pastor it was okay. My pastor back home does not deviate from scripture and I really appreciate that part."

Pastor Rick: "Our pastor seems to present topical messages. Perhaps, I will let him know your feelings."

Donny: "No disrespect meant, Pastor."

Pastor Rick: "None taken. Let's order some food."

The conversation switched to family issues. One thing that Donny and his brothers had in common was they all sang in church. It must have been passed on from his mother since he never heard his father sing a note. That thought triggered another that came three weeks after his father's conversion. Donny recalls asking God for a sign that his dad's salvation was real. Confirmation came when his older brother shared about spending the day with dad and something strange happened. Dad started singing. He never heard him sing before as well but it was what dad was singing that warmed his heart. "When the Roll is Called up Yonder" proceeded out of his father's mouth. Pastor Rick noticed a wry smile on Donny's face. His curiosity led Donny to share that account. Later, he thought about that moment as if it was another one of God's seeds being planted. Throughout his life Donny had past events or thoughts come and go. Later, he would see the fruits. Was this one of those times? Was there something in Pastor Rick's life that needed closure? Time would tell.

Donny continued sharing details about his son and daughter. Grandchildren seemed to take center stage. Donny agreed to continue the conversation at the pastor's house in a nearby retirement community.

> Pastor Rick: "This is home. We love it. No stairs to climb or lawn to mow."

> Donny: "It's beautiful. I think your wife has tended the flower garden, which is gorgeous."

> Pastor Rick: "That's her specialty. Glad you noticed. Come on in. I have something that I have longed to share with you."

> Donny: "Okay. I can't wait to hear what that is."

> Pastor Rick: "Do you remember creating the P.E.P. program at church?"

Donny: "Yeah. It stood for People Encouraging People. What about it?"

Pastor Rick: "That is the one program that has endured over the years. It is a line item in the budget, but never has funding allocated."

Donny: "What do you mean?"

Pastor Rick: "Anonymous donations come in regularly. As people have been touched, they or family members are moved to support the program. It's a pay it forward concept so to speak."

Donny: "That's so great to hear."

When the P.E.P. program was first initiated one young family needed encouragement. Their starter home needed new siding. To save money, the husband removed the deteriorated and worn-out shingles, which were piled in the back yard. The new siding was professionally installed but the old shingles were an eyesore to neighbors after the winter snow melted. Donny was called to help stack the shingles by the road for garbage collection. The pile had to be limited to a fixed height and width. The task was done but hardly made a dent in the rest of the shingles that remained. Donny contacted his brother who had a friend in the garbage business.

A large container was dropped off at the home. About a dozen people from the congregation arrived at the home the following Saturday. The shingles and an old dilapidated shed nearly filled the container. An elderly neighbor had several fallen limbs in her back yard, which were cut and added to the bin. The whole process took less than two hours. Those who lacked the strength to carry the shingles served beverages that were supplied by other church members.

The homeowner's wife took the pulpit at church the following day to share her thanks. She went on to share that several neighbors came over in appreciation for seeing the mess cleaned up. When they asked how the work was accomplished so quickly, the response was "Members of my church did it." The neighbor's response was "What church do you attend?" At least one neighbor was in attendance that morning as a result.

The concept is pretty simple. Whenever a need is presented, willing people are contacted to meet the need. Often, that only requires manpower. Materials like paint or hand tools are provided. It is amazing how quickly a yard can be cleaned up, a broken handrail repaired or other services when tasks needed would solicit volunteers. Those skilled in the trades, like electrical, plumbing or carpentry are especially useful. Tutoring in math, science, computers and other areas can lift a parent's spirits for a child less able to perform in class. Some people made financial donations to help pay for materials and other needs. When young couples were unable to attend restaurants, concerts or other events requiring funding, these monies were used to encourage them as well.

Pastor Rick: "Several homes have been painted by the P.E.P. program over the years for shut ins."

Donny: "That's great."

Pastor Rick: "A lot of the youth have been involved and enjoyed it."

Donny: "Passing skills down to the children is wonderful. I think I failed in that area with my son. I tried but he didn't like to watch me work. Hand tools took on a new meaning when placed in his hands."

Pastor Rick: "Painting those homes had an even better reward."

Donny: "What do you mean?"

Pastor Rick: "Family members would notice the new look during visitation and inquire with their loved one about how it happened. The idea that a group of people would donate time and energy like that further encourages hearts. Many of them added to P.E.P. donations."

Donny: "I sure hope that the P.E.P. project continues for a long time."

Pastor Rick: "People need encouragement, so I am sure it will."

Donny: "Hearing You share about the P.E.P. program has lifted my spirits."

Pastor Rick: "I hope we can get together again before you leave. I have more to share."

Donny: "I will be here next week, but you better get on my schedule. I think I will be pretty busy."

Pastor Rick: "How about Tuesday morning. Can I meet you somewhere for coffee?"

Donny: "Pick the time and place and I will be there."

They exchanged phone numbers and set the meeting. After enjoying a warm slice of homemade apple pie, Donny shared that he had to go. He desired to spend more time with the pastor but promised another therapy session with Jason.

Coming back home was a great idea, based on that news. In order for the P.E.P. project to survive all of those years, people needed to be constantly aware of their surroundings. Many may have passed by a home in need of a paint job or a yard needing a good clean up. But, when people begin to get involved they no longer see just trees.

The Coffee Shop

When Donny arrived Jason had a table cleared and ready for a game of gin. For him it was no longer considered therapy.

Jason: "I am ready for you, bro."

Donny: "You feel lucky?"

Jason: "Let's see. Cut the cards."

The first game seemed to dash Jason's hopes as he found himself doing a lot of dealing. Donny made the normal remarks referring to it as therapy. They both enjoyed the rhetoric. Before long they were playing a third game to establish the two out of three-game winner.

Donny: "Looks like the therapy worked. You won,

bro."

Jason: "The week should offer more opportunities. So how was church today?"

Donny began sharing the events of his day. Jason remembers helping to get a load lugger dropped off at the house for the couple. His friend had since retired from the garbage business.

Jason: "That must have been great news for you Donny. You always seemed to enjoy helping others."

Donny: "I really didn't think it would last. That was one of my passions. Usually, someone must step up and take the lead."

Jason: "You mean that no one replaced you?"

Donny: "Somehow people just seemed to enjoy helping others, especially teenagers."

Jason: "That's amazing."

Donny: "My thoughts exactly. Imagine a child asking

his parents if he or she could help someone in need."

Jason: "That never happened around my house."

Donny: "Cutting grass, raking leaves, or mowing the lawn was definitely dad's job at my house as well."

Jason: "So what do you think made the difference?"

Donny: "Pastor Rick said that when something was scheduled, like leaf raking, young people saw it as a fun way to get together. Then when they saw the smiles it created they also smiled."

Jason: "So, we should have scheduled our mundane tasks as a group event, huh?"

Donny: "That's where we went wrong."

They chuckled.

Donny: "Where would you like to go for dinner?"

Jason: "I picked up those hot dogs that you can't get in Georgia. Erica made potato salad. How's that sound?"

Donny: "You don't have to twist my arm, bro. I'll get the grill going."

As Jason wheeled the grill out to the patio, Jacob came back with his mom. He ran to his papa with excitement. The two seemed to have a special bond.

Jason: "How was your day Jacob?"

Jacob: "Mommy and I went to the zoo today papa."

Jason: "Did you have fun"

Jacob: "I really like the giraffes. They have really long necks."

Jason: "That's so they can eat the leaves from tall trees Jacob."

Jacob: "Yeah. They sure must eat a lot of leaves. They are big."

Jason: "We are going to have hot dogs tonight. Are

you hungry?"

Jacob: "I always have room for a hot dog Papa."

Jacob left to change clothes and wash up. The smile on Mary's face said it all. They had spent quality time together. Donny came out to light the fire and continued sharing about the day's events. The thought of eating hot dogs and potato salad seemed like a fitting end.

One of Donny's desires during this visit was to patron a small coffee shop that he regularly visited prior to going to work. At first he made the stop to ensure that his family would enjoy hot showers in the morning. The electric hot water heater would not replenish fast enough and cold water would not be pleasant for someone. He would leave more than an hour before anyone else would arise solving the problem.

Donny: "Is that coffee shop on Dewey Avenue by the railroad tracks still open for business, Jason?"

Jason: "I don't go that way very often, so I am not sure. Why do you ask?"

Donny: "I spent twenty years visiting there around

six in the morning during weekdays. I wonder if I would recognize anyone today."

Jason: "We could check it out if you like."

Donny: "It has to be early. Can you leave before six?"

Jason: "No problem. Even though I am retired, I still get up early."

Donny: "Tomorrow it is then."

The next morning came and off they went. Upon arriving, the shop was still there with some noticeable additions. It used to hold only a few tables and a countertop with bar stools. Twenty or twenty-five people would fill the establishment, although there were rarely more than ten at any moment. The new expansion seemed to indicate that a full crowd might be close to a hundred. The parking area was larger and several vehicles were there. Upon entering only the counter area looked familiar but it wrapped around into a larger room with many tables. Donny saw two counter stools open near where he used to sit and the two sat down.

Owner: "Can I help you?"

Donny: "Black coffee and one of those Danish for me. I'm buying, bro."

Jason: "Coffee with cream and a Danish for me as well."

Donny: "It has been a long time since I have been here. I think more than thirty years. Joe used to be the manager. I never knew his last name."

Owner: I took over this place twelve years ago, but a woman had run it. I don't remember anyone named Joe."

Donny: "Did you expand the place?"

Owner: "The deli in the back was added two years after I took over."

Donny: "So how's business now?"

Owner: "We are open longer with a lot of take out. Business is great."

Donny: "I think Joe closed after lunch but he had a large morning take out. My company used this place for refreshments in many early morning meetings."

Owner: "Eastman Kodak was a great customer but corporate downsizing has taken a big toll. We still have a large clientele but from small businesses, schools and a few churches."

The coffee arrived and the conversation ceased. Jason seemed to take everything in stride. After tasting the Danish both brothers smiled. Then a man sitting at a corner table stood up and walked towards them.

Man: "Donny. Is that you?"

Donny: "That's my name. Do I know you?"

Man: "My name is Jack. Jack Belcher. You changed my life."

Donny did not recognize the face but the voice sounded very familiar.

Donny: "How did I change your life Jack?"

Jack: "You were the first person who ever spoke a word to me. I sat at the end of the bar." (Jack pointed to the stool)

Donny: "Jack? That must have been twenty-five or thirty years ago. I remember a man, but he had a heavy beard."

Jack: "Yeah, I was that man. My wife of twenty-nine years had me shave it off after we wed."

Donny: "I sure don't remember you married, so that must have happened after I left."

Jack: "You shared your faith and even prayed for me on many occasions."

Donny: "That sounds like me, Jack."

Jack: "I had been coming here for about a week when you showed up. No one said a word to me before but you did. Do you remember what you said?"

Donny: "No, but that does not surprise me. I enjoy

meeting new people."

Jack: "Are you having a good week?"

Donny: "I am."

Jack: "No. Those were the very words that you spoke. It was Friday and I must say that my week was not good. You changed all that Donny."

Donny turned to Jason with a look of wonderment. Throughout his life, Donny found himself saying the exact words to a stranger that seemed to inspire hope or joy. He was drawn to people. They were not trees.

Jack: "I don't think I would have come back to that coffee shop if you had not greeted me that morning. It was like a sign or something. Anyway, every morning afterwards I returned with the hope of seeing you."

Donny: "I must have left before your marriage. Tell me about that, Jack."

Jack: "I learned a great deal about you in our daily

conversations Donny. You had a comforting spirit, and I always felt encouraged. You shared your faith and tried to lead me to Jesus."

Donny: "I am pretty transparent that way."

Jack: "After you left, I missed our conversations. I started attending a local Baptist church where I met Julie."

Donny: "Julie? Is that your wife?"

Jack: "She sure is. Your words had a deep impact on me. I accepted Christ as my Savior, have been baptized and live the Christian life with joy today."

Those words caused Donny to leave his stool and give Jack a warm embrace. He had planted seeds that fell on good soil. Silently, he paused to pray and thank God for allowing him to be part of a greater plan. Jason seemed to feel the emotion as well but kept silent. Visiting the coffee shop that morning was like another divine appointment. Donny felt God's presence and could not wait to hear Jack's story.

Donny: "So we need to talk further. How long do

you usually stay here?"

Jack: "I have to leave in a few minutes but can you be here tomorrow?"

Donny: "I can. See you tomorrow Jack Belcher. Now I know your last name."

After Jack left, Donny shared the experience with Jason on the way home. Although, Jason was not involved in the conversation, He sensed the joy on his brother's face.

Donny: "Coming to the coffee shop brought back some fond memories. I did not know what to expect but felt the urge to revisit that place."

Jason: "That was quite a visit, bro. You have always been willing to openly share with people and I can see that as a blessing. I am not like you in that way."

Donny: "That's not me, bro. A wee small voice in my head seems to place just the right words in my mouth."

Jason: "God uses you for sure."

Donny: "God uses anyone, even you Jason. I think I have been sensitized to that voice."

Jason: "You will have to tell me all about your visit tomorrow morning."

Donny: "So, you aren't coming with me?"

Jason: "You know the saying, 'Two's company and three's a crowd.'

Donny: "You are more than welcome bro."

Jason: "You need to share together. Besides, I might be tempted to eat another one of those delicious treats and my waistline can't take that."

The two brothers smiled with agreement.

The Follow Up

Donny had thoughts about his trip north with a true sense of excitement. God had given him glimpses of how his life had impacted others. The P.E.P. program was still working at his church. Jerry Thompson and his family are serving the Lord. The thought of hearing all about Jack's changed life was uplifting. Then he remembered Pastor Rick's desire to meet with him about something else on Tuesday, which was the next day. Donny tried to reflect on all that was happening and smiled.

Jason: "What's that grin on your face all about bro?"

Donny: "I must have been daydreaming. This trip has been really special."

Jason: "Jacob may have already left for school but Mary might still be home."

Donny: "Don't tell them about the Danish. The girls might get upset."

Jason: "They might at that but not because we didn't bring them some. I might get the third degree about fat calories."

Donny: "Mums the word bro."

Donny picked up his cell phone and sent a text message to Pastor Rick to set the time and place to meet. He shared that he would be tied up between six and eight, but lunchtime would work well. Pastor Rick quickly responded and a lunch date was set at a diner near the church. Before heading south, Donny met with a group of men regularly for prayer on Friday mornings. The diner served breakfast for them afterwards. Donny had fond memories of those men and the fellowship. After all those years he wondered if a waitress would still work there. Their friendship on those Friday mornings was also special.

The lights were on when they returned to Jason's home. Erica was having coffee alone. Mary and Jacob had left for work and school.

Erica: "Home already Honey?"

Jason: "The place was still there but we didn't stay long."

Donny: "It had expanded but still had some of the familiar looks."

Jason: "Donny met an old acquaintance."

Erica: "Wow! That must have been something after all those years."

Donny: "That's an understatement. His name is Jack. I didn't recognize him at first but he knew me. We are meeting again in the morning. His life has taken a wonderful turn with Jesus at the helm."

Erica: "I can see the joy on your face Donny. You'll have to share more."

The rest on the morning was just that. Tears of joy, hugs and smiles could be witnessed by anyone who might visit. There is something about a single soul's salvation, which touches heartstrings. Jesus said it this way:

Luke 15: 3-7 (KJV)

3. And he spake this parable unto them, saying,

4. What man of you, having an hundred sheep, if he lose one of them, doth not leave the ninety and nine in the wilderness, and go after that which is lost, until he find it?

5. And when he hath found it, he layeth it on his shoulders, rejoicing.

6. And when he cometh home, he calleth together his friends and neighbours, saying unto them, Rejoice with me; for I have found my sheep which was lost.

7. I say unto you, that likewise **joy shall be in heaven over one sinner that repenteth**, more than over ninety and nine just persons, which need no repentance.

Although, Donny had no details to share, Jack's words and demeanor spoke volumes. Somehow, Donny's words had changed Jack's life. Donny could not wait to sip coffee with Jack in the morning. The rest of the day included several silent prayers of thanksgiving. God got the glory.

Donny set his alarm for an early morning rising. His internal clock woke him minutes before the alarm. The anticipation of hearing Jack's life changing experience would not allow him to sleep further. Jack had not arrived when Donny entered the coffee shop. A corner table with two chairs looked inviting. Donny thought that the morning conversation might get emotional, so the table seemed to be a better choice than the counter stools. Donny ordered coffee and sat down. Jack arrived shortly afterwards holding a small bag. He spotted Donny and walked over to the table.

> Donny: "Good morning Jack. Can I offer you something from the counter?"

> Jack: "I hoped to buy yours but black coffee would be just fine."

Donny went to the counter to get the coffee while Jack placed the bag on the floor and sat down. By the time Donny returned Jack had removed a picture and placed it on the table. Donny could see that it was a family photo.

> Donny: "Here's your coffee Jack. Is that your family?"

> Jack: "That it is my friend. I thought I would start with the present."

Donny: "You have a beautiful family there. I do not have many pictures with me but we can still share about family."

Jack talked eloquently about his two daughters, a son and his wife Julie. One of his daughters was married with two children. It seemed as though the grandchildren in both lives took center stage. They were like trophies given for success. Perhaps, they were as both families followed Jesus. The two men shared many events that demonstrated Christ's handiwork. It was obvious to Donny that jack's conversion was real and he wanted to learn more.

Donny: "Jack, yesterday, you shared that something I said or did thathad an impact on your your life. What did you mean by that?"

Jack: "I cannot say that it was anything you said. Rather, it was how you lived."

Donny: "How I lived?"

Jack: "You were genuinely concerned about whatever I was going through in my life. You were authentic and personal. When you left I felt something missing.

Donny: "Did you figure out what that was?"

Jack: "I knew that you had something different. Your faith in God was evident in how you interacted with people, not just me. I saw you purchase items for complete strangers and later shared that you were, somehow, led to do that. "

Donny: "That wee small voice in my head seems to guide me a lot."

Jack: "That's just it, Donny. I never had that kind of leading. I started attending a church near me. The first sermon seemed to pierce my heart."

Donny: "What was it about?"

Jack: "The Comforter."

Donny: "You mean the Holy Spirit Jack?"

Jack: "Yeah! The pastor's message seemed to be meant for just me."

Donny: "That's how the Spirit works my friend. The message may have pierced many hearts but those who hear think the way you did."

Jack: "I met with the pastor later that week to share my thoughts and feelings. I wanted the Comforter to come in and fill the void that I felt after you left. It was as if God wanted you to leave to open new doors for me."

Donny: "I am sure that you were part of His plan all along. He is the 'Alpha' and 'Omega.' He knows the beginning and the end. He even knows us before we are born."

Jack: "I am sure that's true but how do we prove it?"

Donny: "It's in His Word."

Donny began to share several verses of scripture including:

Ephesians 2:10 (KJV)
10. For we are his workmanship, created in Christ Jesus unto good works, which God hath before ordained that we should walk in them.

Revelation 1:8 (KJV)

8. I am Alpha and Omega, the beginning and the ending, saith the Lord, which is, and which was, and which is to come, the Almighty.

Jack: "That really explains a lot, Donny. The pastor led me in prayer for my salvation. Admitting that I was a sinner was tough. I thought I was a good person. All I knew was that I wanted what you had."

Donny: "We are born sinners."

Jack: "I accepted Jesus Christ as my personal savior that day. Then new doors began to open."

Donny: "Tell me more."

Jack: "I was invited to a men's bible study. There I met several men like you with a genuine passion for serving the Lord and helping me grow in Christ. They prayed for me, helped me through tough decisions at my workplace and more."

Donny: "I still have men holding me accountable."

Jack: "That's a great point. Accountability was what I needed."

Donny: "What other doors opened?"

Jack: "I learned about spiritual gifts. Yours is definitely encouragement."

Donny remembered Pastor Rick's similar comments. He had often denied that he had such a gift. His childhood was filled with trauma. If anyone needed encouragement he did. It took a long time to learn that God uses many of the experiences that we encounter early in life to mold us. Just as Donny felt the lack of encouragement early in his life, his sensitivities to others were heightened. Ephesians 2:10 is a constant reminder of that.

Donny: "So, Jack, what do you feel is your gift? When you accepted Christ the Holy Spirit lives inside you. He is the gift giver."

Jack: "One of the men in my small group gave me a test and it showed servant hood. I think that is true as I enjoy helping others. That is how I met Julie."

Donny: "This I gotta hear."

Jack: "I worked as a cabinet maker. My carpentry knowledge also helped in home repair. Julie had shared with one of the men in my group that she desired to expand a room in her home. That involved removing a wall. After receiving her phone number, I called and introduced myself. She did not live far from me, so I agreed to stop on my way home from work that very day and provide a quote. I hoped that it was not a load-bearing wall as that would be expensive."

Donny: "How quickly did that happen after you gave your heart to Jesus?"

Jack: "The next week. It was incredible. Anyway, I stopped at her house to assess the job and Julie came to the door. She looked familiar. After brief introductions, she shared that she was a member of the same church that I attended."

Donny: "Another God thing my friend."

Jack: "That's for sure. I think she thought I was a hippy or biker by my rough looking beard by her first reaction. My first impression of her was much better."

Donny: "Don't tell me that it was love at first sight."

Jack: "Okay, I won't. She just seemed so upbeat. I mean that she welcomed me with pleasure. My appearance may have said something else but she saw me like a longtime friend. It's hard to describe but I loved it. Before she showed me the wall that she hoped to remove, she offered me a drink. I didn't expect that. I respectfully refused and reviewed the work. My price was accepted, and the work was done the following weekend. It was not a difficult job, but would require additional follow up with floor repair, that I offered for free."

Jack went on to share that the beard was shaved off that very night. He was a completely different looking man when he showed up to perform the work. Jack made several trips back to complete the floor repairs. During the process, Julie shared things about her family, friends, and pet cat called "Pepper," named after his black and white spots. Neither of them had ever married, but both were animal lovers. Meetings at church, meals together and other events began to join their hearts. The work was accomplished to Julie's delight.

As a new Christian, Jack shared that he prayed for the right mate to share his life with. The men that he met with in the prayer group were all married and often shared uplifting moments involving their wives. It was something that touched Jack's heart and he desired the same kind of experiences. Spending time with Donny in that coffee shop may have served to meet a similar need in the past but he desired someone new. Julie had been praying for a mate as well and God took care of the rest. They were married on their one-year anniversary of that first meeting. Jack shared that their first daughter was a product of their honeymoon coming about nine months later.

Jack pulled out a framed document from the bag and showed it to Donny. At first, he thought it was their wedding information but Donny read the word "Baptism."

Donny: "Tell me about this, Jack."

Jack: "Before we were married, we talked a long time about faith. Neither of us had been baptized and were naïve to the concept. We discussed it with the pastor, who assured us that it was not a requirement for salvation. He talked about Jesus seeking public acknowledgement of our conversion. We agreed that when Jesus came into our hearts everything changed. We were not ashamed and desired to be baptized in the church. That happened before we were married and to this day may have set the tone for the rest of our blessed life together."

Donny: "That's quite a story Jack. Don't be afraid to share it."

Jack: "Like most couples we have our ups and downs, but God gets the glory."

Donny: "Amen my friend. Amen. I hope all this sharing hasn't made you late for work."

Jack: "Not at all. I put in for a day's vacation. I figured this time would not be short and I needed to share these things with you. Like I said before, you changed my life."

Donny: "God did that. He may have made me an instrument but rest assured, you were on his heart and mind from the beginning."

Jack: "No doubt about it."

The two men continued sharing for another hour. It was as if two long lost brothers met for the first time after many years apart and needed time to catch up. Both were uplifted. Donny shared how God had been with him while he led his father back to the Lord at age eighty-nine in a nursing home, along with several other divine appointments. Those attending the coffee shop may have witnessed hugs and tears of joy. Perhaps, even their lives were affected.

Rick's Meeting

The stay at the coffee shop seemed short but Donny realized that the time had slipped by. Pastor Rick may have been waiting at the diner as Donny hurried to meet him. Fortunately, the diner was only a few minutes away. Once again, Donny felt tremendous joy after talking with Jack. Anticipation added even more positive feelings as he drove to meet Pastor Rick. The diner looked the same as it did thirty years ago as he pulled into the parking area. Pastor Rick was there waiting at a corner booth.

Pastor Rick: "Over here Donny."

Donny made his way to the booth. Pastor Rick was his usually upbeat self, although the years had taken their toll. He still had a full head of hair but silver had replaced the more familiar brown hair color.

Donny: "I hope you haven't been waiting long Pastor. I just had a wonderful reunion with an acquaintance from my past."

Pastor Rick: "Just arrived Donny. I haven't had time to order lunch. You will have to tell me more about your meeting."

Donny: "I hope you have a lot of time to spare, Pastor."

Donny smiled. The waitress took their orders and Donny began to share about the morning's experience. Pastor Rick kept the conversation going with a genuine interest. Whatever he had to share would wait. Donny's joy was infectious.

Pastor Rick: "Not many people get to see the fruits of their labors Donny."

Donny: "What do you mean Pastor?"

Pastor Rick: "You have been a great encourager to me over the years. Obviously, you have used that gift in that coffee shop."

Donny: "I remember you telling me that when I was

a young father. I didn't believe that I had that gift until much later."

Pastor Rick: "You may remember sitting in many church meetings as my guest as well. I desired your input even though the meeting may not have been of interest to you. Still, you came and I so appreciated it."

Donny remembered some of those meetings. He would understand if they had anything to do with church maintenance, as he performed electrical, plumbing and other tasks on a regular basis. He also remembers those not associated with his skills.

Pastor Rick: "Do you remember when I asked you to sit in the monthly meetings involving church leadership?"

Donny: "I remember the agony. Every month we kept falling further behind in visitation. The lady who headed that commission reported that many new people had come to the church but no one had come forth to head visitation needs."

Pastor Rick: "I remember how you handled that situation."

After almost a year of hearing the same report, Donny took command of the meeting. He was tired of hearing that someone had to come forward to chair the visitation needs and offered a solution. He suggested a pancake breakfast to be held in the fellowship room near the kitchen. He would recruit some teenagers to help with the cooking and service needs. Then he told the assistant pastor attending the meeting to invite all new visitors and mix them with regular attenders. He suggested that they interact through word play games. The next monthly meeting came with the words, "We are all caught up."

Pastor Rick: "Your pancake breakfast had even more benefits. Do you remember the teenagers who helped?"

Donny: "I remember Tony and Steve, specifically."

Pastor Rick: "A few months before that breakfast, I asked you to work with a few wild teens on Tuesday evenings. Our regular midweek programs needed help. You agreed."

Donny: "They were good kids. Tony had poor eyesight but desired to be a chef. I let him cook sausage and pancakes."

Pastor Rick: "Tony is one of those people that I wanted to share about. His eyesight never improved but he completed chef training in New York City."

Donny: "Wow! That's amazing. Do you know where he is now?"

Pastor Rick: "He still cooks with his wife's help not far from here."

Donny: "So he's married too. I need to check out the place where he works."

Tony's poor eyesight was the result of his mother's drug problem. Tony had been removed from her care when she went into incarceration. A church's foster care family took him in and later adopted him. Pastor Rick shared that if Donny had not spent time with Tony, he may well have gone down the same dark path as his mother.

Pastor Rick: "The time spent with Tony on those Tuesdays and at your home had a profound impact on his life."

Donny: "I also benefitted. He would cook for us on those evenings. He made lemon chicken to die for."

Pastor Rick: "That's what I am talking about. Tony had a dream and you encouraged him to follow it. You would not let his poor sight be a setback."

Donny did not have a fixed agenda on those Tuesday nights. He let the teens decide how they wanted to use that time. Tony suggested cooking so Donny provided food supplies. The other teens enjoyed working in the kitchen as well. On many occasions, Donny brought Tony to his home for a meal and additional share time. Tony seemed to enjoy movies with a dark theme, violence, bad language, etc. Donny would agree to watch some of them with Tony as long as he would be willing to discuss the movie afterwards. Donny noticed that Tony had a change of perspective afterwards.

Donny never felt comfortable working with younger children. He may have said no to Pastor Rick if that option was presented but young adults fit Donny's comfort level.

Donny: "Pastor, I enjoyed spending time with those

teens, especially, when it meant stimulating their minds."

Pastor Rick: "Tony said that you showed him how to become a millionaire."

Donny: "I remember that. It was a lesson on compound interest."

Pastor Rick: "Tony was impressed and said that he was following your leading."

Donny: "I wish our school systems would teach practical things like that now."

Pastor Rick: "I wish I was in your class. I am working on my second million. I gave up on the first. (smiling) So, tell be about your teaching."

One night, Donny gathered the teens around a blackboard and asked if they would like to be millionaires someday. When they responded with some excitement, Donny continued the discussion by asking if they ever heard about "The power of seventy-two." That lesson was about using their youth years to build a substantial nest egg when they retired. The power of seventy-two was defined like this:

Divide 72 by the prevailing interest rate.

That result is the number of years an investment would double. Then Donny brought a chart of the Savings and Poor (S&P) from inception. Donny took a span of about fifty years earlier and showed the average interest gained on the S&P was over 10%. He used 12% because it equally divided into 72 to illustrate.

Then he said, "Suppose you are sixteen and starting a minimum wage job. Since you live at home, you could easily invest twenty dollars a week.

Now suppose that you did that for five years and stopped. You would have invested five thousand dollars. At twelve percent, you would have accumulated over eight-thousand dollars at the age of twenty-one.

At age 27 you would have $16,000. (first 6-year period)
At age 33 ...$32,000
At age 39 ...$64,000
At age 45 ...$128,000
At age 51 ...$256,000

At age 57 ...$512,000

At age 63 ...a million dollars.

The teens were impressed, but Donny continued with a new question for the teens:

Donnie: "What if you did not invest when you were young and started at age forty-five. Then you saved a hundred. dollars a week. (approximately $5000 / year). Who would have the most money for retirement?"

Donnie: "They answered incorrectly, thinking the $5000 would catch and pass the teen who only invested $5000 total. As the chart earlier shows, the teen's investment was at $128,000, At age fifty-one, the man who started late would have less than $50,000, while the teen's funds were still more than five times that amount."

Pastor Rick: "You are so right Donny. They should have taught us that in school."

Donny: "The teens and I had thoughtful discussions. I was happy to be a part of their lives."

Pastor Rick: "That time spent has paid dividends for those youths and took a burden off my shoulders as well.

They shared other memories together. Reminiscing those by-gone days was special for both men. Donny thought about the trip north and seeing his pastor friend again. He would not have learned about some of the blessings that he heard presented. He thought that most people do not get the chance to understand how their lives may have positively affected others. The decision to drive north was a blessing and more than he expected.

The meeting triggered several thoughts about the two youths that Donny spent time with. Knowing that Tony was married and enjoyed his passion of cooking was special. Pastor Rick did not share a lot about Steven but indicated that he did not recall any problems. Steven graduated high school and moved away. Donny hoped that he had also turned to Jesus as Lord.

Pastor Rick prayed with Donny and thanked him for the wonderful lunch. Donny could sense the joy in Pastor Rick's heart, perhaps like the father when the prodigal son returned in Luke's parable (Luke 15). It had been over sixteen years since the two men had seen each other. That was at his wife's funeral. This was the first time they had the time to share together. Donny had a special place in Pastor Rick's heart and ministry. That message came across loud and clear.

The Old Stomping Ground

Donny enjoyed spending time with his old friend and reflected on the meeting. He smiled as he thought of Tony fulfilling his dream of becoming a cook. Knowing that he had a wife added to his pleasure. He often wondered if someone would be there to help him if his eyesight failed. Without knowing the rest of the story, Donny offered a brief prayer for Tony and his family for continued joy, peace, success and happiness. Donny remembered when Pastor Rick asked him to work with some troubled teens all those years ago. He had a willing response, yet he felt unprepared. He left the agenda to the Lord. Now he had a glimpse of how God had used him. Someone once said that God doesn't care so much about a person's ability, but rather, their availability. Donny made himself available to serve.

The diner had not changed significantly from those Friday mornings with the men's prayer group. He did not recognize any of the waitresses as they were all young. The older servants used to greet the men with tables ready. Usually, they knew what each man would order and other information. Donny remembered asking a waitress, named Amy, about her husband's golf game. She always said that Donny should play with him sometime but that never happened. Her husband could have turned professional according to her responses. Donny wondered if that ever happened. Reflecting on people that cross our paths is a part of life that may not show results but can bring a measure of joy in our lives. The diner did just that for Donny.

Donny had not driven through his old neighborhood during this visit and felt the urge to do that. It was about five miles north. As he approached thoughts of friends and neighbors began to fill his mind. He knew that his neighbor Ed had passed away several years ago but wondered if the home was still in the family. Ed's daughter lived there and cared for her father during those final months of his life. Ed worked at a local brewery and peddled flowers on weekends with his brothers. He also enjoyed making doll houses from scraps of wood discarded from the brewery. He loved keeping his yard mowed and pleasing to the eye.

The subdivision looked the same except for the much taller trees. Donny stopped in front of Ed's house and noticed a few familiar sights. Ed had a wagon with a young girl pulling it as a yard decor. It was made of wood. The girl wore a red dress, red shoes and a flowered hat. The wagon was still there but the colors were badly faded. Still, Donny thought that the home might still be in the family, so he knocked on the front door. A young lady answered.

Lady: "Can I help you?"

Donny: "My name is Donny. I used to live next door."

She called her mother to come to the door.

Mom: "Donny? It's Christy. Remember me?"

Donny: "Of course I do Christy. "

Christy: "What brings you here today?"

Donny: "I decided to take a trip up to my old stomping grounds. It is so good to see you."

Christy: "Likewise. Come on in."

Christy began to share about her mom and dad at great length. It was as if she had so much to talk about. She had raised three children and was now a grandmother. Her two failed marriages left her as a single parent. Her mom and dad helped her through most of the tough times and she missed them. Donny was like a breath of fresh air. He knew that her father had a form of dementia in his last months and was a burden for her. Still, she talked about caring for him with love and affection. She wasn't sure if her father would have recognized Donny, if he was alive, but remembers one phrase that he said over and over before he passed. It was "Rare irises." Donny knew instantly what he was referring to and began to share.

Donny: "One Mother's Day weekend, your dad was selling his flowers on his usual corner. As you know I loved to help him, especially on holidays."

Christy: "You helped him a lot Donny. Dad loved having you there."

Donny: "He always desired for me to pray before any flowers were put on display. On slow times we talked about Jesus and I read scripture to him."

Christ: "Mom and dad started going to your church."

Donny: "That they did. I am confident that they both accepted Jesus as their personal Savior as well. Your father prayed for salvation on one of those flower corners."

Christy: "I believe they are in heaven as well."

Donny: "Anyway, the term 'Rare iris,' came from me."

Christy: "Go on."

Donny: "Ed had been making the same flower combinations for a long time. He had some purple flowers that were different from the rest I told him to make a larger bouquet with one of those flowers in the middle."

Christy: "When I helped my dad, he had five-dollar carnations, six-dollar mixes of carnations with daises. Then he would add a single rose for seven dollars."

Donny: "You remember well Christy. He also would sell six roses together with garland for eight. When I told him to add a rose and the purple flower to the six-dollar carnation combo to sell for ten dollars, he laughed. He said it would never sell for so much."

Christy: "That would be like my dad."

Donny: "Nevertheless, he made two dozen bouquets like that."

Christy: "So what about the "Rare iris?"

Donny: "When the crowds came Ed was in the back making bouquets as fast as he could, while I tried to tell the customers the pricing. Carnations are five dollars, these are six, seven with a rose, and...Then I stuttered to describe the ten-dollar bouquets. I did not know what the purple flowers were called so I said something like, these with the rare iris are ten dollars."

Christy: "So, what happened?"

Donny: "All twenty-four bouquets sold out before the customer line ended."

Christy: "That must have really surprised dad."

Donny: "It sure did. He didn't believe that he could get ten dollars for a bouquet for one thing. Then when the crowd was gone, he came out laughing hysterically. He stuttered 'Rrrrrare iris.' Then said that he grows them in his back yard."

Christy: "That explains it. I would wheel him outside and he stared at the purple flowers, which really are irises though not rare. That day had a profound affect on him."

Donny: "After that, he always had ten-dollar bouquets for sale, especially on holidays. One day we dropped off several buckets of those arrangements with one of his brothers who needed flowers on his corner. Ed told his brother that we were getting ten dollars. His brother said that he could not get that on his corner."

Christy: "What happened?"

Donny: "He sold out both buckets within a half hour."

Christy: "That must have surprised him as well."

Donny: "Ed and his brothers started selling flowers

with their father and kept the tradition long after he died. If I wanted to buy flowers for someone special ten dollars would have been expected, especially if it were a holiday. Making change would be simplified as well. Your father learned those lessons. Did he tell you the story of the painted weeds?"

Christy: "I don't remember that one."

Donny: "Ed would buy differed colored spray paints like red, blue, green and yellow. He liked bright colors. Then he would collect dried thistles and spray them. Usually, he would add one or two to a flower arrangement. Customers would often pay an extra dollar or two."

Christy: "I remember dad doing that."

Donny: "He would also put several of the thistles by themselves as an arrangement and sell them for four dollars."

Christy: "I also remember seeing those buckets in the garage when he returned. I guess he didn't sell many."

Donny: "That may have been true, until I came along and changed the way he presented them."

Christy: "What did you do?"

Donny: "Your dad would cut the thistles all the same length so the tops would be even across. I took one bucket and rearranged them to look staggered like they grew in the fields. My bucket sold out immediately."

Christy: "Dad never told me that story."

Donny: "Maybe not but he staggered those weeds afterwards."

Christy: "One thing that dad did share often before he started with his dementia was when he had his knee operation."

Donny: "Oh yeah. I told him not to worry about the lawn mowing. I would take care of his lawn when I did mine."

Christy: "Dad loved his yard. While he was recuperating, he would show signs of anxiousness until he heard your mower running."

Donny: "He couldn't stop talking about that at his retirement party."

Christy continued sharing about her family and the neighborhood. One neighbor still lived across the street. Another family was divorced and moved away. The family that bought Donny's house had recently moved but the new owners seemed friendly. The street was clean and orderly. Donny was glad to have made the stop. Somehow, he felt that Christy needed that time as well. Perhaps, God designed the meeting with another purpose. Donny prayed for Christy and her family and drove back to his brother's house.

Cranberry Pond

Memories stay with us long after we retire. As Donny drove out of the old neighborhood some of them began to fill his mind. Those weekends with Ed on his flower corner brought a smile to his face. Ed was a great neighbor and friend. Donny remembered many times when flower sales were slow, and Ed wanted him to open God's word. As Donny read, Ed would ask questions. Often, that would stimulate further study. Sometimes, the two men would laugh when they pictured themselves as characters in the study. Those moments were special. Donny remembers the day when Ed accepted Christ as his savior on one of those quiet times and it warmed his heart. Someday, Ed would greet him at Heaven's gate, perhaps with a rare iris in his hand. Donny smiled as he started back to Jason's home.

Jason lived on the shore of Lake Ontario. If you went due north across the lake for about fifty miles you would arrive in Toronto, Canada. Before Donny left the state a Ferry boat would take passengers and their cars across the lake, but now the ferry ride was gone. It would be a three-hour drive through Niagara Falls which Donny had visited with his family on several occasions. The view from the Canadian side was spectacular and invited millions of tourists around the world every year. Lake Ontario overflowed into Lake Erie through the majestic Horseshoe Falls. Donny thought it was one of God's master pieces of creation. Memories of those visits began to surface as Donny turned onto the road along the lake.

Then three ponds on the opposite side of the road caught his eye. The first was Long Pond, followed by Buck and then Cranberry. Jason's home was soon after. Donny pulled off the road at Cranberry Pond. He walked down the stony shore near where his father took him and his brothers fishing many times. There was something about that spot that intrigued him. Dad would always catch the most and biggest fish there. Donny and his brothers rarely caught anything. Dad spent more time untangling their snagged lines than his sons did fishing. When dad pulled out a fish Donny remembers tossing his line in that spot. Dad would tell him to find his own place to fish.

The ponds were fed through tributaries from Lake Ontario. On this day the water was noticeably low. As Donny looked down into the pond he could see the top of something about a foot below the surface. It appeared to be rectangular, like a large box. It was about twenty feet off the shore. Those fishing trips with dad seemed to be at that exact spot. Then things began to make sense. Dad must have known about that sunken crate as the hole it made may have attracted fish. He would cast just beyond it with a float on his line to avoid entanglement. The bigger fish hoovered there. Donny's attempts to cast there would result in more snags than fish.

Donny couldn't hold back a smile as he thought about those days so long ago. Most of those fishing trips occurred while living on that side of town. Donny was not a teenager yet. Of course, dad knew where the biggest fish were. He knew what was below the water. He knew how to set the float at the precise height to allow the bait to fall just after the buried obstacle. That knowledge needed to be shared with his sons if they were to catch the big ones, but it also required the skills to perform the best cast. That would take time. Still, dad enjoyed those times with his sons along with those fish dinners.

In the winter months the ponds would freeze over. Fishing through holes in the ice could be done but the catch was not as predictable. Donny recalled many cold days alone with his father on the ice. Dropping the fishing lines with baits was easier than casting. When Donny pulled up a nice perch his dad beamed with pride. He also would take the fish off the hook for his son, which was greatly appreciated. There was something about spending time with dad that warmed both hearts. Donny's thoughts began to shift towards his own family. Did he have those intimate times with his son and daughter? He did take them fishing on those ponds when they were young. By the time they became teenagers those times became fewer and fewer.

Donny recalled another day during the winter when the ponds were frozen. He was about thirty and started playing golf. On that day he stopped along one of the ponds and placed a golf ball on a tee made of snow. Then, facing the pond, swung a nine-iron striking the ball. It flew high and about a hundred yards onto the ice. Then Donny watched as it bounced more than a dozen times. Donny never saw it stop. Later, it became a golf story for his friends. He told them that he once hit a nine-iron over a thousand yards. That would have been unbelievable until he shared that it was on ice.

Reflecting at Cranberry Pond brought many smiles. When he arrived at Jason's home, he shared those memories with the family. Jason also remembered fishing with dad, snagged lines and more. They laughed together.

Jason: "So how did your meeting go with your friend at the coffee shop?"

Donny: "Fantastic. Jack shared his testimony and we talked for more than four hours."

Jason: "Wow. You did a lot of catching up."

Donny: "I guess you could say that. Thirty years is a long time."

Jason: "That long, huh?"

Donny: "Jack told me that his life dramatically changed after he met me."

Jason: "I heard him say that. So, tell me more, bro."

Donny: "He said that it wasn't so much as to what I said, but how I lived. He sensed something different in me and wanted it for himself. I told him that what he sensed was God's spirit working in me."

Jason: "So then what?"

Donny: "He started attending a local church, accepted Christ as his Savior, married a Christian lady who attended and more."

Jason: "That must have made your whole week."

Donny: "You can say that. Then I had lunch with Pastor Jack."

Jason: "I remember you telling me that you were going to do that. It has been a busy day for you already."

Donny: "It sure has. This has been a great trip. Are you ready for your therapy session?"

Jason: "Therapy, nothing. You are going down, bro."

The table was cleared, and the cards were dealt. Donny could not help sharing more about his day. Jason was more than willing to hear the details.

Witnessing

J ack's testimony resonated in Donny's head all day. God had
used Donny in that coffee shop so many years before without
his knowledge. That was not unusual. Jack's joy in talking about
his changed life was so uplifting that Donny wondered about his
own life story with others. Jack shared that Donny's life impacted
him, but Donny never shared his testimony with him. He had giv-
en his testimony during church events but he could not remember
doing so in a setting like Jack did. He wondered if he should have
shared it with Jack that morning. The time went by so quickly, that
it might not have been possible. During a moment of prayer, he
sought God's leadership.

Scripture tells us to always be ready and willing to give the reason
for our faith.

1 Peter 3:15 (KJV)
*"But sanctify the Lord God in your hearts and be ready
always to give an answer to every man that asketh you*

a reason of the hope that is in you with meekness and fear."

Donny interpreted that verse as sharing his testimony regarding his salvation. Jason had a testimony that prompted a new discussion.

Donny: "Have you ever shared your testimony, bro?"

Jason: "What do you mean?"

Donny: "I remember your televised interview on 'The 700 Club' after you recovered from your skiing incident. That was very moving."

Jason: "Maybe it was for you, but I was pretty nervous."

Donny: "That might have been from the cameras and lights. Still, you have a great testimony to share about that experience. God was with you in a big way."

Jason: "I have often asked, 'Why me God?' I am a living miracle."

Donny: "Everything about that trip seemed to be planned in advance."

Jason: "What do you mean?"

Donny: "Prior to that vacation, Erika shared that the two of you were having some marital problems. Was that true?"

Jason: "I had bursts of temper on occasion. I did not know why, but I think my tour in Viet Nam may have messed up my brain. I was always sorry afterwards but my tantrums troubled Erica."

Donny: "She shared that on the TV interview. She also shared that you were a changed man after you recovered. I think God did a miracle of restoration on your brain while in that coma."

Jason: "I think so, too. Those outbursts slowed and diminished in intensity. We now enjoy being grandparents together."

Donny: "The helicopter rescue had been initiated

that very day as well. You were airlifted almost immediately. That was no accident."

Jason: "I was their very first rescue. After I came out
of the coma one of the EMTs came to see me in the
hospital. He also called me God's miracle."

Donny: "See. That's what I am talking about. You
need to share that experience with the world. That is
a great testimony."

Jason: "I have shared that story in church a few times,
but not recently."

Donny: "You might have found it easier to share with
friends but what about strangers? When God opens
a door for you, you need to enter."

The brothers continued to share many things about God's love
and care over the years. Donny shared about the doors that were
opened in his life. Some of them were not entered immediately yet
God persisted. There was always a sense of joy that followed when
God's will was followed. The fact that the creator of the world
would use people to accomplish His work was amazing. Biblical
examples like Moses, David, Jonah, Ruth, and many more became

part of the discussion. By the time dinner was ready, both brothers agreed that they needed to be more open to God's leading. Perhaps, even in retirement, God had more doors to open.

Before retiring for the night, Donny reflected on the whole day's events. He was overwhelmed and prayerfully thanked God for the enlightenments. Somehow, the message from the pulpit so many years ago came alive. "They're Not Trees." If Jason would share his testimony with others, he needed to see them as God does. To Him they are not trees. He knows their inner soul and desires restoration. Jason's ski trip was part of God's plan for restoration in his family relationship. Donny was convinced that it was also for future witnessing.

Donny reflected on his childhood that was marred by the loss of a mother, followed by years of foster homes. His brothers were reunited with their father and new mother during grade school. During those early years, parental love was lost and it had a profound affect. Donny thought about Pastor Rick's observation that he had the spiritual gift of encouragement. At the time, he thought that if anyone needed encouragement, he did. Then he realized that God used his childhood experience to help others. His older brother seemed to have the gift of teaching. He always searched for "Why" things happened as they did. Jason was the youngest. Perhaps, God was using Donny to access his gifts. One thing was certain. Spiritual gifts are given to produce fruits for His kingdom.

One Last Stop

Donny spent the next day with Jason and his family. His son came over that evening with his wife and three children, two sons and a daughter. As he talked with them and observed their relationships, Donny was impressed. The oldest son was home from his first year of college. They were excited to see their uncle and share about where they were in their lives. One thing came across loud and clear. They knew the Lord. Jason's life may have been his witness. His son knew first-hand about the ski trip and the miracles that followed, which may have been shared in detail with his children when they were old enough to understand. They were a loving Christian family.

Donny shared with them a deeper thought about his mother. Her Jewish heritage was something special when he learned later in life that it made him Jewish by descendance as well. Her conversion to Christianity made her life even more special. When she knew that God was about to take her home, Donny was certain that her prayers went out for a reunion in Heaven with her entire family.

Her husband, three sons, their families and at least one more generation were prepared to join her. Donny reflected on that thought and smiled. Coming home was a great idea. It may have been a prelude to an even greater joy in heaven.

Before going to sleep, Donny was overwhelmed again by the day's events. Sharing about his mother to a new generation seemed to prompt new thoughts. The story of Moses leading the Israelites across the Red Sea came to mind. It did not take many generations before they forgot what God had done for them. They wandered for forty years and were kept from the Promised Land. Donny knew the importance of sharing what God has done in his life as well as family history. His advice to Jason to share his testimony may have come from God as well. Then he felt a sadness come over him and a new thought. "How many people leave this world without ever knowing they were loved? That might have happened to him. He bowed his head and prayerfully thanked God for the constant reminders that He was always there for him. Jesus addressed his disciples in the last two verses of the book of Matthew with these words: (27b-29)

> *"All power is given unto me in heaven and in earth. Go*
> *ye, therefore, and teach all nations, baptizing them in*
> *the name of the father, thy Son, and of the Holy Ghost:*
> *Teaching them to observe all things whatsoever I have*

*commanded you, and Lo, I am with you always, even
unto the end of the world. Amen"*

Although he was not one of the original disciples, he knew that
was a command given for all believers.

Thursday morning came with a brilliant sunrise. Lake Ontario's
glasslike water seemed to mirror the sunlight. Jason and Donny
enjoyed the view over a cup of coffee. It was a special time for them
both as they spent the day trying to get caught up for all the lost
years that they had missed. Jason recalled a recent visit to Georgia
when both of his brothers had a reunion. They made a two-hour
trip north to do some gem mining in North Carolina. Although
everyone got dirty, lasting memories were formed. The experience
was one that needed to be revisited in the future. The day seemed
to fly by as the two brothers shared together.

The week was nearly over, and Donny prepared for his return
trip. The next day had a few more things planned to include a fish
fry and a custard. Joshua decided to join him for the day as well.
The original Abbott's custard stand was located near a beach on
the lake about a twenty-minute drive away. Next to the stand was
a familiar restaurant, called Char Broil, known for their ground
beef burgers with all the trimmings including a hot sauce topping.
Donny recalls a time when he took his wife, son and daughter for

dinner. His son was nine or ten at the time with a good appetite. After finishing his burger, he was still hungry. Donny remembers filling a small paper cup with hot sauce and told his son that it was vegetable soup. After a small spoonful, his son rushed to a nearby drinking fountain. "You got me dad" were the words spoken after finding relief. Over the years family pranks were enjoyed. Donny smiled, soliciting a response from Jason.

Jason: "What are you grinning about, bro?"

Donny: "Remember the vegetable soup story?"

Jason: "Vegetable soup?"

Donny: "I told my son that the hot sauce at Char Broil was vegetable soup and he took a spoonful"

Jason: "I remember. At first, I thought it was mean" (but he laughed afterwards)

Donny: "If you mention that place to my son today, he will still smile. It was one of our good memories. He is over fifty now and we still laugh about things that we recall from the past."

Jason: "That is special. My kids enjoy reliving stories as well."

Donny: "You have been blessed with a terrific family. I enjoyed spending the evening with them last night."

Jason: "Thank you. Grandkids are our reward."

Donny: "You got that right."

Jason: "So what do you have planned for your last day here? Of course you are welcome to stay longer."

Donny: "Lunch at Char Broil sounds like a good start. Then we could walk down the pier on the lake."

Jason: "I suppose that would burn off enough calories to have a custard afterwards, huh?"

Donny: "You don't have to twist my arm. First, you need some therapy, bro."

Jason was up to the challenge and cleared a table. The cost of the custards was on the line. Brotherly wagers were a normal part of the game over the years. Bragging rights became part of their comradery. Donny was able to pass the challenge and still offered to buy the cones, but Jason said it was the least he could do as payment for the therapy. They both laughed.

At noon they left for the restaurant. Donny shared that this day would spike his metabolism and his diet would begin on his drive south. The beach was at the bottom of a steep hill with the restaurant on the left near the end. An inlet from the lake was lined with cement walls on both sides. Two quarter-mile piers extended out into the lake from both sides of the inlet with lighting for night walks. Donny recalled fishing from the pier with his father and later with his son. Even when they were not catching fish, everyone enjoyed the walk. Often, they watched other fish being caught as well. At the end of one pier was a small lighthouse that was used to warn sailors of danger when storms approached.

The Char Broil looked the same as he remembered it. The menu looked the same but the sign appeared to be new. Donny smelled the odor of onion rings which were handmade and delicious. They placed their order, took a number and sat down. When the burgers came, their jaws dropped. The burgers extended well outside the buns, while the added toppings made them look more like a tower. Stretching one's mouth far enough was a problem that they took pride in accomplishing. A single order of rings was shared as it could feed a family. Another memory was being made from the trip.

The walk to the pier was now welcomed. The first building they passed was the custard shop. Donny shared a memory about the time when his wife and sister-in-law purchased a cone prior to walking on the pier. After the walk they decided that enough calories were burnt off to have another cone. The burgers took away that urge for Donny and Jason. It was a beautiful partly sunny day. Clouds looked more like cotton puffs that offered occasional relief from the hot summer sun. People lined both sides of the pier with metal fences and ropes keeping them safe. Most of the fishing seemed to be towards the channel side. Stopping to see if any fish were caught made the walk slow and rewarding.

All different sized crafts travelled within the channel, from small motorboats with fishing rods to fifty-foot-high sails carrying sun worshippers. Donny enjoyed the walk and was glad that he remembered to grab a hat. Jason's bald head was already red and he might feel some added discomfort when he showered later. Donny offered some sunscreen that he took from his golf bag and spoke about the dangers of skin cancer. One of the inherited characteristics that came from our mother was baldness. All her brothers had hair loss on their scalps. Dad had a full head of white hair when he died, but his sons only grew hair on the sides. The last time Donny walked the pier was with a full head of brown-colored hair. The years had passed but the pier provided fond memories.

The walk took over an hour. At the end of the pier was a small amusement park. Donny recalls watching his children sliding down the slides, swinging on the swings and spinning on the wheel that required dad's help. In the distance was a merry-go-round that appeared to be well-maintained. Donny used to ride it with his children when they were young. Jason still takes his grandson there on occasion after enjoying a cone. The older we get, the more we enjoy those special memories in our minds. Abbott's custard is one of those.

Jason: "We are here, and I lost. So, what's your pleasure bro?"

Donny: "If they have chocolate almond, then I will have one scoop in a waffle cone."

Jason: "You are in luck. It's today's special."

Donny: "My lucky day. Chocolate almond and you're buying."

Jason: "My pleasure. This has been a good day for me as well."

The cone was devoured rather quickly as the sun and warmth of the afternoon accelerated the process. Before leaving, Donny purchased some pints to go. On the way back they stopped at a grocery store for a few more items. Zwiegels hot dogs and Grandma Brown's baked beans headed the list. Florida and North Carolina now had the hot dogs and custard for sale in a select few places. Like the custard, Zweigle's hot dogs became must have items during any visit. The uniqueness of the hot dogs came in two forms. Both had natural-casing skins that would pop open during grilling. Somehow, that seemed to add a special flavor. The beef ones were red in color while the other variety was pork. They were white-colored. They came six to a package with other quantities available. Donny had placed ice packs from a cooler in Jason's freezer to keep three pounds of each cold. In addition, a large basket of wax (yellow) beans was purchased for the trip back.

When they arrived home, Erica spotted the Abbotts bag with a smile. Jason shared a few details of his day, while she prepared a small treat for herself.

Jason: "We are going to play cards on the deck. Enjoy the custard."

Erica: "I will. Thank you."

Donny: "I hope everyone will join me for another fish fry around five."

Erica: "Mary should be home and I don't plan on cooking."

Donny: "Great."

The therapy session ended the afternoon's activities. They only played two games and each won one of them before it was time to leave. Mary and her son arrived in time as well, so off they went. The restaurant was only ten minutes away. During the ride, Jason shared about the trip to the beach with his grandson who smiled. Although he might have wished he was there, he seemed to sense the joy in his papa's heart. Donny also sensed the bond that the two of them had.

Leaving the restaurant left Donny full and sad. He never found a place that served fish fries like Upstate New York. The beer-battered crust made the large cod filet melt in his mouth. Fish in the south appeared to be small and made from frozen pieces. The filet that he just ate hung over both sides of the plate and was smothered with potato fries. A cup of slaw completed the meal. A few restaurants served the meal on other days, but Friday was always a treat.

The Return Trip

S pending the week with Jason and his family was a blessing but it was time to head south. Donny did not want to wake anyone early the next morning, so he made his final greetings that evening before retiring. He carefully packed the ice chest and was on the road before five for the fourteen-hour drive. The sun did not rise until he was well into Pennsylvania where he stopped for breakfast.

The restaurant was a familiar one that he frequented with his father several times on their return trips. It overlooked the beautiful mountains that glittered with flashes of sunlight on the trees. Donny recalled those fall trips when the splendor of God's creation was evident with brilliant colors. It was a masterpiece. Ordering eggs with home fries seemed natural as he recalled past visits at that place. They knew how to cook potatoes unlike any place in the south. The orange sauce they were cooked in gave a welcome taste that he had not experienced for a long time. Memories of his dad enjoying the same meal popped into his head and warmed his heart. The thoughts of his dad seemed vivid and detailed.

Donny was overwhelmed by all the memories that resurfaced during this trip. The human brain is so amazing and far beyond any computer devised by man. It could store continued events through the eyes. Even more amazing was the fact that they could be recalled half a century later with such detail. He reflected on God's design and how people could possibly believe that it happened by pure chance. How could the number of image pixels stored over a lifetime be stored in the size of a fist? That thought gave Donny a pause. He thanked God for being so wonderfully made. Psalm 139, verse 14 said it so well. *"I am fearfully and wonderfully made."*

Donny remembered a time when he visited his sister-in-law's parents on a dairy farm in New York. Her dad had retired and talked about how quickly the time had passed ever since. He had worked from early morning till sunset all his life and now lived a life of leisure. He retired to his favorite chair after lunch only to wake up three or four hours later. He wondered where the time had gone. Donny recalled sharing with him that we take in events our entire life and later recall them as memories when we are older. Her dad agreed with that. He said that he could remember things that were over fifty years old, but not what he ate for breakfast. Donny was at that point. Those times with his father seemed to come alive with each familiar setting. The restaurant reinforced that.

After receiving a cup of coffee to go, Donny continued south. The road was not a divided highway but carried many rural settings. Horse and buggy signs indicated the Amish presence who lived simple lives. Donny and his wife purchased bedroom furniture from a similar sect called the Mennonites in Upstate New York, which still was in use in his home. The workmanship was superior to that found in furniture stores. Working with wood was one of his favorite hobbies, but he could never compete with the quality that he saw firsthand when he visited an Amish site. He recalled huge saw blades driven by extra wide belts and pulleys. They were primitive compared to his ten-inch table saw. The tools used to carve and shape the wood looked like something from the old west. Yet, they did a masterful job. Donny wondered if they had caught up to the twenty-first century with modernization. Somehow, he hoped that they had not.

The thoughts of those visits seemed to pass the time as he reached Virginia where the modern highway appeared. Although he could make much better time, the straight three-hundred-mile route to North Carolina seemed to take forever. There was something about the winding roads and hills that offered relief for the long drive. The occasional rest stop helped to break the trip up along with new caffeine, but without hunger pains. The eggs and home fries seemed to do the job.

Donny continued to scan license plates for new states as if his father was travelling with him. When he passed a field with horses or a graveyard, new memories surfaced. During those summer fishing vacation trips to the Thousand Islands, dad would play a game with his sons. Whenever anyone would spot horses, they needed to shout, "horses." The first to shout would total the number of horses in view with white ones counting double. The number would be added to their account. The person with the most horses at the end of the trip would be declared the winner. There was never a prize associated, just bragging rights. The catch came when a graveyard was spotted. Then, "Bury-em" needed to be shouted. The first to do so kept their horses, while everyone else started over. Donny never knew where that game started, only that his dad always won. He knew where the graveyards were. Donny recalled playing that game with his children but the alphabet game had more appeal. Still, horses and graveyards triggered special memories.

The return trip filled Donny's mind with other thoughts. At the start of his trip north he was apprehensive. The thoughts of those fish fries and custards seemed like good things but he felt a higher satisfaction by the people that he met. Pastor Rick provided information that spoke volumes about God's presence in his life. Many people go through life without knowing that their life made a difference in the world. The P.E.P. program seemed to do that for recipients and workers. Tony was fulfilling his dream in the culinary field. Jerry was living a Christian life with a loving family.

God had directed so many events in Donny's life without his awareness. This trip brought him to that realization and provided a sense of tremendous peace. At the loss of his wife Donny was filled with so many "Why?" questions that were directed towards God. Silence was deafening in his empty house, causing a morning routine that led him to local coffee houses. Was that part of God's plan as well? After his wife's passing Donny began to recall many events that involved meeting new people and started writing them down. The common bond between them involved changed lives. Some readers referred to them as "Divine Appointments." Donny's life began to make sense. The "Why?" questions were answered. He may have tried to turn away but his heavenly father was always by his side directing his paths. He silently uttered a prayer of thanks as he drove.

Then Donny recalled the coffee shop meeting with Jack. Replaying his story made the time fly again. Donny could not comprehend how God had used his life as a witness as Jack stated. He could not remember his initial meeting with Jack. He only knew that it made a profound difference. No one had approached Jack before and he almost stopped going to that shop. Only God could have known Jack's thoughts or feelings. The Holy Spirit was at work prompting the conversation between the two men. Donny may never had known that without making this trip. He thanked God for the insight. He also wondered if the Spirit had more to do through him. Being used in that way is a special privilege. The results can lead to great joy in Heaven. Donny thought about a reunion with his parents and other loved ones as well as with those who were placed in his life along the way. The trip north provided a glimpse of what that might look like and it warmed his heart.

North Carolina provided more memories. One vacation brought several families together in a cabin that slept twelve. Donny's daughter left with a marriage proposal as her boyfriend came along. Donny's son also brought his girlfriend who became his wife. Donny's older brother came from south Florida with his family. Dad was delighted to join everyone after losing his wife the year before. The timing now seemed perfect. It was the last time dad would see everyone before his stroke. Only Jason's family was missing. Memories of that vacation began to resurface as Donny drove past the route that led to the site.

Donny laughed as he remembered the pranks that his wife played on her best friend. He recalls her attempts to speak a southern drawl and her sister-in-law's response in kind. Neither of them had mastered the concept but they laughed until their sides split. Three generations enjoyed playing cards together. The first evening began with a campfire, guitar playing and songs. Before the sunset on the next day, Donny recalls his dad gathering wood for the fire. The night before was very special to him. Donny did not remember hearing his father sing but reflected on the joy that he saw in his father's face around that fire. It was a memory that Donny wished he could have over. Getting family together in that way again became a new bucket list item. What a joy it would be to add Jason's family in such a setting.

The I85 interchange in Charlotte meant that he had three hours to go. He wondered where the time had gone. He was happy to see that he had missed the rush hour traffic which was part of his reason to leave early. It was rare to make the long drive without some kind of delay, like an accident or road work. That did not happen. Donny hoped that the rest of the ride remained equally free of distractions. God may have read his thoughts as he arrived home less than three hours later.

The ice chest was still cold and had done its job well. The dogs were carefully repackaged in smaller ziplocked bags and placed in the freezer, except for a few for the weekend. He had picked up some grocery items prior to his arrival that included potatoes, whole milk, and hotdog rolls. The memory of his dad cutting those yellow beans triggered a desire to prepare the same delicacy that evening. This time the sun was still shining. He rarely purchased whole milk, but he remembered his father insisting that it was a must for the best results. A large pot was filled with water and placed on the stove with the burner on high. The yellow beans were then cut into small pieces about an inch long. Then several large potatoes were trimmed and cut. By that time the water was at full boil and the items were added.

Donny set a timer for five minutes and began stabbing the potatoes with a fork. It was a scene that played back in his mind when he watched his father prepare the meal. He knew that when the potatoes were soft the beans were done as well. At that time, he drained the water and added a quart of milk, a quarter pound of butter, salt, and pepper. Then he placed the pot on the stove on low heat. When the butter was fully melted, the taste test was made. To Donny it was to die for. He had talked about the concoction with friends who could not picture it as a source of delight. On a few occasions over the years some would try a taste and like it. There was something special about yellow beans that made the difference and Donny rarely found them in the south. When they were available and friends or family came to visit, they would be welcomed with joy.

There was something about a favorite meal from the past that carried special memories. Yellow beans, potatoes and milk did that for Donny. As he enjoyed the meal, other thoughts began to pop into his head. His wife had worked for a bakery before they were married and learned how to make a flakey pie crust unlike anything you could purchase. When his son was a teenager, he would try various apple pie slices at church socials and respond, "It's not like mom's." Donny always knew what he meant. The apples may have been cooked to perfection, but her crust made the difference. Now, in his fifties he tries to follow mom's recipe to the letter and comes close. It was one of his fondest memories as well as having seconds on the yellow beans and potatoes.

Donny also ate a second bowlful. There was enough left for at least two more meals which Donny looked forward to enjoying. He knew that the recipe came from grandma who had to survive on meager means. Meat was a premium. Donny recalls conversations with his dad about the simple pleasures he enjoyed growing up. To him that meal was a luxury. Although from the world's perspective, dad grew up in a poor family, he seemed to disagree. To him, this meal was better than any steak dinner. Of course, those times when his son paid the bill steak was a joy as well.

Placing the large bowl of leftovers next to the hot dogs brought a smile to Donny's face. It was like an exclamation point to the trip.

He knew that the next few days would have welcomed reminders as well.

The Letter

Perhaps, it was the warm milk that allowed Donny to fall fast asleep. Usually, after a long drive, Donny needed to unwind before retiring. That was not the case as the next morning came quickly. Donny did not remember performing the tasks of brushing his teeth or putting on pajamas but both had occurred. The sun shone through his bedroom window brighter than usual. He was not used to sleeping late and would have arisen much earlier. Still, he was excited to realize that he had a restful night's sleep. A cup of coffee was all he needed as the evening meal kept the hunger pains away.

The thoughts of his trip were still on his mind. It was as if his life had flashed before him through the old acquaintances of his past. He began to understand just how God had used him without being aware. He did not remember the words that he spoke to Jack in that coffee shop so long ago but was able to see the results. Most people go through life never knowing if they had made a difference. God had opened his eyes and he gave thanks. Before leaving on his trip he hoped to see family and old friends but God had so much more planned. Those road signs brought back instant memories that became precious about his father. They were like messages from heaven that all is well. Donny reflected on these things all morning.

The sound of the mail delivery truck was near and he went out to meet it. A stack with mostly advertisements was wrapped by a rubber band and topped with the card that he had filled out to stop the mail during his travel. He laid it on the kitchen table and proceeded to dip a large bowl of his evening meal for reheating. The pangs of hunger had surfaced and the fridge seemed to be calling him. As he sat down to enjoy the treat he removed the band from the stack of mail. Some of the junk mail was set aside like fast food coupons while others were placed in a a separate pile as trash. Bills were set aside as well. Then a letter appeared from Pastor Rick. He quickly devoured his lunch and opened the letter.

The envelope was postmarked on that Thursday after their meeting. It arrived just two days later. Donny had mailed cards to his brother that usually took a week to arrive, so the date stamp was surprising. Seeing Pastor Rick after all those years was a special blessing. The last time there was any conversation was at Donny's wife's funeral at the church. Visitation at his house and having lunch together were highlights of the trip. He couldn't wait to open the letter which read:

Dear Donny,

It was such a pleasure spending time with you to-day. Your presence brought back many fond memories. Thank you for coming and I hope I will see you again someday. You have been in my thoughts and prayers for a long time. When you left for Florida to minister to your dad, I was sad. You were such an encourager to my wife and I. When the news came that your dad accepted Christ, we knew that God had you in his loving care.

I contacted Tony after our conversation, and he wanted to pass on some things to you as well. I will email his information to you so that you might contact him. Anyway, Tony wanted you to know some things about his life. First, he accepted Christ shortly after high school. He wanted you to know that you made a huge difference. You truly cared for him. Second, he has been happily married for twenty-six years with two daughters and a son. One of his daughters still lives at home and works occasionally in the restaurant which

*has been doing well. Third, all his children have good
eyesight, which he is so thankful.*

*He also said that he keeps in touch with his cousin Steve
who is also serving the Lord, I thought that you would
enjoy the update. I am so glad that I asked you to work
with those troubled teens. You made a tremendous impact my friend.*

Sincerely,
Pastor Rick

The tears seemed to instantly flow down his cheeks as he read
those words. He could not hold them back. The letter seemed to
put an exclamation mark on the purpose of the trip north. God
wanted him to know that his life had made a difference in the
lives of people. Most people go through life never knowing that
fact. The gift of encouragement had paid tremendous dividends in
Donny's walk. Donny didn't know that he had that gift for most
of his years, even though Pastor Rick reinforced it.

For the rest of the day, Donny reflected on all that happened.
He couldn't wait for Pastor Rick to email Tony's information so
he could contact him directly. He thought about those days after
his wife passed and the coffee shop escapes to avoid the loneliness.

It was now evident that God used him in those places as well. God was directing his life while he was unaware. Now that was confirmed and he wept even more.

It has been said that life is a blink compared to eternity. A century is certainly a miniscule measure when compared to millions of years. Yet the thought of making an eternal difference during a lifetime weighed heavy on Donny's heart. Not only was a life lived short but he was like a spec of sand on a beach. God uses ordinary people to accomplish extraordinary results. When the shepherds told Mary that she would deliver God's son, she pondered those words in her heart. (Luke 2:18-19) That would happen in the future. Perhaps, she had similar thoughts and feelings. Donny did not know where life's journey would take him. Now he knew that he was not alone. God had been with him all along.

The letter was not very long but left a powerful image in Donny's heart and mind. The fact that it arrived so quickly had additional significance. It was like God's punctuation mark on his life. He placed the letter in a plastic sleeve for protection and put it in a metal box with other important documents. One of them was his Florida baptismal certificate. That reminded him of his father's salvation on the same date. It seemed like wherever he turned God was reminding him of the Pastor's message. Donny was in His loving care. Though he was living in an empty house, he was not alone. That thought brought great comfort.

Final Reflection

P astor Rick's letter placed an exclamation mark on Donnie's life. Making a difference in the lives of those teenagers was a true blessing. He enjoyed those times and hoped that they would go on and lead rewarding lives. The timing of the letter seemed to have special significance as if God had passed it through the postal service with special treatment.

Donny contemplated more details about his relationship with his father. The various road signs that he saw while making the trip were wonderful reminders of the bond that they had together, but dad's salvation took centerstage. Donny began to relive his father's life and all that led to that special day. He learned a lot about his father's early life from his grandmother. Her husband died from lung cancer in his forties. He was a heavy smoker. Donny's dad had to leave before high school to help care for his mother. He remained at home until receiving his draft notice at the age of thirty.

Donny could not get his dad to talk about the war but remembers hearing him say, "There are no atheists in foxholes." Grandma had instilled a heavy dose of her Christian faith in her children. It helped get her son through those tough times in Africa and Normandy during the war. Letters from his sweetheart and occasional pictures also helped. Two purple hearts got him an early release when the war ended and life began anew.

The 1945 World's Fair in New York City put an exclamation mark on their union and wedding bells quickly followed. Mom's Jewish heritage did not pose a problem as she converted to Christianity soon after. She was an orphan who received a fully paid college tuition and graduated with honors. She had secured a prestigious position with a fortune five-hundred company. She was the breadwinner in the family. Their first son was born about nine months after they married. Donny and Jason followed soon after.

Then disaster struck. Brest cancer took mom's life, leaving dad without a job, bankrupt and penniless with three young sons to care for. His prayers for healing were unanswered. God may have been felt in foxholes, but he felt abandoned now. That was not going to happen where his sons were considered. Despite the financial setback, he was determined to keep them together. Family did not step up and foster care was limited.

A one room rental in an undesirable area was all he could afford after securing a low paying job in a machine shop close by. Without a car visitation with is boys was limited until he met a woman who helped him get on his feet. After five years of several foster homes, we finally became a family again. By that time, dad had replaced a relationship with God with activities like reading, puzzles, bridge playing, stamp collecting and billiards. Playing the game of bridge was especially important as it was one thing that he and mom did together before she passed. He had won the honorary title of life master and had a host of people wanting to be his partner.

After retiring to Florida, his second wife died. He continued playing bridge several days each week. Missing a date was unusual but after missing a second one later that week left his playing partner suspicious. The apartment superintendent was contacted to open the door of dad's apartment. They found him unconscious with a head wound but alive. He was rushed to the nearest hospital in a coma. The doctors determined that he had a stroke three days earlier.

God had not abandoned him. All the things he enjoyed were gone. He knew that he played cards but not how. He saw words but could not understand them. The only thing that was still intact was his mind. After relearning how to do simple tasks, like eating, he was placed in a nursing home. That grieved Donny who had taken an early retirement and started his own business in upstate New York.

God called Donny to go to Florida and minister to his father. That meant that he had to close his business and accept a position with a friend in Orlando, about forty-five minutes west of the nursing home. That would allow him to spend weekends with his dad and support himself. Donny's daughter was expecting their first grandchild and his wife needed to stay in New York. Donny initially thought the time would be short and everyone would be together again.

Each trip to the nursing home included sharing about Jesus, which dad seemed to reject. Donny's older brother would make the three-hour drive north from south Florida on occasion and witness as well. Getting dad out of that home was a welcomed relief, nevertheless. Dad had delusional moments like winning the lottery or owning a business that countered any spiritual conversation. Still, dad welcomed those times of visitation with open arms.

After fourteen months of visits a breakthrough occurred. After loading dad's wheelchair in the back of the van, he shared that he would not stay as long as usual. He planned to be baptized by his pastor in the Orlando area that afternoon. That day the chair also held the large print Bible that his sons had given him with the hope that he could read it. Donny placed the Bible on his father's lap.

Donny: "Are you reading it, dad?"

Dad: "I try."

Donny: "Is there something that I can help you with?"

Dad: "All I know is that I want to go to heaven as I know that is where my sons are going to be."

Donny's jaw dropped. Those words penetrated his heart with great joy. God had allowed his dad to survive three days alone after a stroke for this moment.

Donny: "Do you know how to get there?"

Dad: "No."

Donny: "First, you need to understand that we are sinners."

Dad: "I didn't do anything wrong."

Donny: "Oh, really. Have you ever held a grudge?"

Dad: "Oh, yeah."

Donny: "Ever got angry with someone?"

Dad: "Oh, yeah."

Donny continued with other similar questions that had the same response.

Donny: "Consider the maker of heaven and earth looking down into this van. Do you think that He would accept you in His perfect place called Heaven?"

Dad: "No."

Donny: "That's where you are wrong. He loves you so much that He sent his son, Jesus, to die and take away your sins."

Donny led his father in three prayers asking for forgiveness, recognizing that Jesus was raised from the dead and making Him Lord of his life. Each prayer was made by his father in his own words.

Driving back from that nursing home was so emotional that Donny missed his turn to go to the baptismal site. He called his wife who heard his tears of joy. Then he called his brother with a similar result. God gave him the words that led his father to the Lord. Yet, he couldn't help but believe that the baptism had something to do with it. Could it be that thoughts of dad's wife's conversion penetrated his thoughts. At any rate, dad's large print Bible had the date, October 1, 2000, entered with his salvation and Donny's baptism.

God had not abandoned his father. Perhaps, Donny's mom had prayed for her entire family to reunite with her in heaven, and this was the last one on that list. Three weeks later, Donny wanted confirmation that his salvation was real. He was eighty-nine years old with some delusional tendencies. God answered that prayer as well. His older brother made the trip that weekend to spend with dad and shared that something unique happened. Dad was singing in the car on the way back from visiting the local fishing pier.

Donny: "I never heard dad sing, bro."

Brother: "It's not that he was singing that was so strange."

Donny: "Ok, I'll bite."

Brother: "He was singing "When the Roll is Called Up Yonder, I'll Be There."

Donny: "Wow! His mother must have taught him that."

That was all Donny needed to hear. Dad did not make his ninetieth birthday. After the announcement of his passing, Donny's brother left his home to make the arrangements with tears in his eyes. "If You Can See Me Now" started playing on the radio and he felt uplifted. Dad was in heaven. Donny and his brother led the funeral service. His brother spoke about love and joy after playing that song. Donny followed with the same message after playing "When the Roll is Called Up yonder." The message was uplifting with two non-family members coming forward afterwards. The superintendent spoke first.

Super: "I have been a Catholic all my life and I never heard words like that before."

Brother: (after writing key verses down for him to read later) "These are promises in the Bible for you."

Super: "I never read the Bible. The priest reads it to us during service."

Brother: "If you don't have one, I will get a Bible for you."

Super: "I have one. I guess I will start with your references."

Bother: "The book of John is a good place to start as well."

The man left with a new purpose. Our prayers went with him to find a personal relationship with Jesus. Then the lady who played the music came to Donny with tears in her eyes.

Lady: "I have been doing the music for this funeral home for nine years and never heard words like this before. I did not know your father but feel blessed this day."

Donny left to meet family members at a nearby restaurant. He remembers talking to his father with words like:

"Gee, dad. You have only been gone a short time and two people have been touched already."

Donny often tells others that God doesn't care about our abilities but desires our availability. We can fail by our abilities but when we are available to be used by Him, failure is not possible.

Epilogue

When we look at life through our own eyes, we see a dim picture compared to what God sees. We cannot see the future or what it holds. Nor can we understand the past without insights. Donny received a glimpse of both. The Bible spans six thousand years of history from creation to a new earthly kingdom. Those who believe in its truth will enter the pearly gates with a welcomed reunion with friends and family. When God's son Jesus Christ came out of the baptismal waters of the Jordan, the words "This is beloved my son in whom I am well pleased" were uttered by the Father (Matthew 3:17). Donny longed to hear similar words as an adopted son in the kingdom. Perhaps, they were being said through the trip.

www.ingramcontent.com/pod-product-compliance
Lightning Source LLC
Chambersburg PA
CBHW061804120626
46550CB00005B/2128